Demystifying Disability

Demystifying Disability

What to Know, What to Say, and How to Be an Ally

Emily Ladau

TEN SPEED PRESS
California | New York

To Mom and Dad.
Thank you for always riding the
roller coaster with me.

Contents

Introduction:
Why Do We Need to
Demystify Disability? | 1

Chapter 1
So, What Is
Disability, Anyway? | 7

Chapter 2
Understanding Disability as
Part of a Whole Person | 29

Chapter 3
An (Incomplete) Overview
of Disability History | 43

Chapter 4

Ableism and Accessibility | 69

Chapter 5

Disability Etiquette 101 | 87

Chapter 6

Disability in the Media | 119

Conclusion:
Calling All Allies and Accomplices | 141

Further Reading and Resources | 150

Acknowledgments | 157

About the Author | 161

Index | 162

Introduction: Why Do We Need to Demystify Disability?

One billion. More than one billion people around the world are disabled. In fact, we're the world's largest minority. Statistically speaking, there's a good chance this book is relevant to you. To narrow things down a little more, let's do a quick gut check.

- Have you ever tried to talk about disability and found yourself flustered over what words to use?
- Have you ever shushed your kid for asking "what's wrong" with a person who was using a wheelchair?
- Have you ever shared a news story about a disabled person on social media because you felt warm and fuzzy after reading it?
- Have you ever compared yourself to someone with a disability to make yourself feel better about your own life?

If your response was "yes" to any of these, don't stress. I'm not here to judge. Consider this book a safe space to learn and find answers to certain questions you might have but aren't sure how to ask.

It's pretty common for the mere mention of the word *disability* to evoke fear, confusion, and an endless stream of misconceptions. And often, people don't realize their own biases. There's much work yet to be done to change hearts and minds—or, at the very least, to get nondisabled people to stop treating disabled people as a weird cross between precious gems and alien creatures. And I am one of the many disabled people who are passionate about doing such work.

So, a little about me: I have multiple disabilities, including a physical disability, a hearing disability, and mental health disabilities. I use a wheelchair because I was born with Larsen syndrome (LS), a joint and muscle disorder that I inherited from my mom, Ellen, who also has it. You might think that our both having LS is a tragedy, but *we* don't. In my humble opinion, it's pretty fantastic to have someone built into my life who just *gets* me. But I know my mom didn't always feel this way. When she and my dad, Marc, were considering having a baby, they sought out genetic counseling and were reassured that my mom wouldn't pass on LS. Midway through the pregnancy, though, an ultrasound showed otherwise. My mom was absolutely overcome with guilt, fearing the worst for me and worrying that I'd resent her. And even though that couldn't be further from the truth, I don't blame her for these concerns. Society was even less disability-friendly while my mom was growing up than it is now. And once, when I was a baby, a woman was staring at us because she noticed our disabilities, and my mom overheard her say, "Look at what that mom did to her baby." That rude comment left a sting that's never gone away.

Even so, in the years since my birth, there's been a continued shift toward greater acceptance and understanding of disability.

But all of us—nondisabled and disabled people alike—have more to learn about how to make the world a better, more accessible, more inclusive place. So how do we do this? There's a philosophy I've come to embrace that informs everything I do:

If the disability community wants a world that's accessible to us, then we must make ideas and experiences of disability accessible to the world.

How can we expect understanding and acceptance of disability if we aren't willing to share our insights and our stories? I recognize this isn't always a popular line of thought among many disabled people. Educating others about the nuances of your daily life is a heck of a lot of work, and it can take an emotional toll—especially when there's pushback, or the people who need to learn just won't listen. It makes sense not to want to live our lives moving from one teachable moment to the next. We'd prefer to just live our lives, period.

However, the reality is that we're not quite there yet. Whether I'm out and about in the world at large or just aimlessly scrolling through social media, I'm on high alert for ableism, stereotypes, stigma, and discrimination toward disabled people—and there is a lot of it to be found. So, for now, I believe that offering honest and sincere guidance and conversation remains a key part of the path forward for the disability community. That's how progress has been made by the powerhouse disability activists who have come before me. It's how we will continue forward. And if one person who reads this book thinks better of using disability as a slur or insult, or calls their representatives to advocate for a disability issue, or adds a ramp to the entrance of their shop, then we're moving in the right direction.

There's No Test at the End

This book is a 101 on certain aspects of disability for *anyone* seeking to deepen their understanding and be a stronger ally, regardless of whether they identify as disabled. Use it as a reference, a resource, a jumping-off point, or a conversation starter. But remember, this isn't a textbook or an exhaustive encyclopedia of disability. I'm not an academic, and I won't be subjecting you to a pop quiz on what you've read. Instead, I hope that you'll take what you learn from this book and apply it to real-world conversations and situations. And if you don't get your language quite right on the first try, or you still have questions about whether a movie you saw recently represents disability in a positive light, that's okay! I promise this isn't a class that you're going to fail.

The most important thing is that you aren't just reading this book to try to get a gold star for doing the right thing or being nice to disabled people. Including, accepting, and supporting people with disabilities doesn't make anyone a saint. That being said, learning about and understanding experiences outside of your own is a process, so don't be too hard on yourself.

Disability Is Not One-Size-Fits-All

At certain points, I'll refer to the "disability community" as a collective term for disabled people. While we are indeed a diverse and beautiful community, it's important to know that I'm not using this term to erase or gloss over our individual experiences. *There is no singular disability experience, and this book is in no way intended to be representative of every single person with a disability.* We're each our own person, and everyone's thoughts and experiences are different. Because disability exists in infinite forms, even people who share the same diagnosis (if they have one) don't have identical experiences.

My family is a perfect example of this. In addition to my having the same genetic disability as my mom, my Uncle Jonathan has it too. In some ways, our bodies are really similar. We're all shorter than five feet, our thumbs are rounded like spatulas, our elbows are permanently bent, and we all have hearing loss. But we're also each affected differently. My mom and I were both born with a cleft palate (an opening in the roof of the mouth), but my uncle wasn't. Both my uncle and my mom can walk, but I can't. Even with our shared DNA and shared disability, our experiences are unique.

So it's important to remember that if you've met one disabled person, you've met *one* disabled person. And if you have a disability, then the only disability experience you're an expert on is your own. The same logic is true in regard to this book. This is just one book on disability, and while my goal is to shine a spotlight on a wide-ranging spectrum of topics, perspectives, and experiences, please remember that I perceive the world through the lens of a person with an apparent physical disability. There's a whole world of words and wisdom about disability out there. Wherever you are in your journey, whether this is the first thing about disability you've ever read or the hundredth, I encourage you to keep reading, keep learning, and keep going.

Chapter 1

So, What Is Disability, Anyway?

Disability is not a brave struggle or courage in the face of adversity. Disability is an art. It's an ingenious way to live.

— Neil Marcus, actor and playwright

Disability. How does that word make you feel? What does that word make you think of? And what does it mean, anyway? My mom taught me that the dictionary is always a good place to start when you don't know where to begin. Here's what Merriam-Webster has to say:

dis·abil·i·ty | \ ˌdis-ə-ʹbi-lə-tē \ 1: a physical, mental, cognitive, or developmental condition that impairs, interferes with, or limits a person's ability to engage in certain tasks or actions or participate in typical daily activities and interactions.

Then there's the definition found in some major disability nondiscrimination laws. For example, here's how the Americans with Disabilities Act defines it:

The term "disability" means, with respect to an individual,

(A) a physical or mental impairment that substantially limits one or more major life activities of such individual;

(B) a record of such an impairment; or

(C) being regarded as having such an impairment.

While both of these definitions are pretty straightforward, each is centered on what a person can and cannot *do*, which is only one way to think about disability. There are many other ways to define disability that go beyond the narrow understanding of disability as *inability*. We all need to think bigger. So, how do *I* define disability? After years of existing in this body of mine, my definition is *Disability: a state of being; a natural part of the human experience.*

But I'm only one person, so I asked other disabled people to share what disability means to them.

Ellen Ladau, my mom: "Disability isn't static. It evolves, both physically and emotionally."

Cara Liebowitz, writer and activist: "Disability, to me, is a social identity, but it's also about having functional limitations."

Imani Barbarin, writer and activist: "Disability is a holistic experience, so it must have a holistic definition. Disability is not just a physical diagnosis, but a lived experience in which parameters and barriers are placed upon our lives because of that diagnosis."

Jaipreet Virdi, assistant professor, University of Delaware: "As a deaf person, I consider deafness a spectrum; the range of which defines an individual's identity and lived experience. Thus, deafness—and disability more broadly—is an oppression of difference rather than an impairment."

Lawrence Carter-Long, author, artist, and disability media enthusiast: "Once upon a time, disability was just a diagnosis. Thankfully through time, the notion has evolved to embrace broader concepts, like constituency, identity, and culture."

Liz Weintraub, senior disability advocacy specialist: "Disability means that there's something people can't do. I believe that there's something everyone can't do as well as they would like, except that people with disabilities have a label. But I am very proud of my disability, because that's who I am."

So, as you can tell, *disability* isn't just a static term with a single meaning. It's a big, broad term to describe a natural, constantly evolving part of the human experience.

How Should I Talk about Disability?

"One size fits all" is a myth. Yes, I'm looking at you, clothing stores, but really, this applies to so many facets of our lives, including language. There isn't one single way to talk about or think about disability. But—and stay with me here, because things are about to get mind-bending—it's important to *think about* how we *talk about* disability, because the way we *talk* shapes how we *think*, and the way we *think* shapes how we *talk*. Whew!

The choices that we, as disabled people, make about how to describe and define ourselves are deeply personal, and each of us has our own preferences. The way people who have a disability talk about their disability is *their choice*—I cannot stress this enough. We all need to respect these choices, even if we're also disabled and someone else's choices are different from our own. With that in mind, let's talk about talking about disability.

There's one thing we should address right away—we need to stop using the word *handicapped*. It's an outdated term that's fallen out of favor with most disabled people, and, quite frankly, it makes my skin crawl. Occasionally, I'll find myself saying things such as "handicapped bathroom" or "handicapped entrance" because old terminology dies hard. But there are better words to use. Talking about a person? "Disability" is better than "handicap." Pointing out a parking spot with the blue lines? It's "accessible" parking. Now that we've settled that, you'll notice throughout this book that I switch between the terms "person with a disability" and "disabled person." That's partly because I like to shake things up a bit in my writing, but it's mostly because these terms honor two of the main ways of referring to disability: person-first language (PFL) and identity-first language (IFL).

Person-first language (PFL) does just what it says: it puts the word "person" first, before any reference to disability is made. This type of language is all about acknowledging that human beings who have disabilities are, in fact, people first, and they're seen not just for their disability. So when using PFL, you might say "person with a disability" or "person who has Down syndrome" or "people who use wheelchairs." The logic here is that disability is something a person has, rather than who they are, so by separating any mention of disability from the person and putting it second, you're showing that you respect the personhood of someone with a disability.

Identity-first language (IFL) is all about acknowledging disability as part of what makes a person who they are. So when using IFL you might say "disabled person" or "blind person" or "Autistic people." In this case, disability isn't just a description or diagnosis; it's an identity that connects people to a community, a culture, and a history.

Neither of these choices is wrong, though many people strongly prefer one over the other. I prefer IFL, since disability is absolutely part of who I am. But I wasn't always so aware of language and didn't give any real thought to what I called myself until college. A special-education professor put me on the spot during a lecture, asking me to back him up on PFL or bust. I went along with it in the moment, but it made me uncomfortable.

PFL is intended to explicitly serve as a reminder that having a disability doesn't mean one is less of a person than anyone else. When PFL came about, it was a necessary step forward for disability rights. But I struggle with the idea that acknowledging the existence of disability is somehow dehumanizing. You wouldn't go out of your way to call me "a person who is Jewish," right? You'd say I'm a Jewish person. I'd say I am Jewish. You wouldn't say that someone is "a person who is bisexual," would you? You'd say they're a bisexual person. It just makes sense, because these are identities. They describe parts of what makes a person whole.

Truth be told, I went kind of overboard with my IFL evangelism at first. I couldn't understand why anyone would prefer PFL and pushed against it whenever I had the chance. But after a while, I had a revelation. My dislike of PFL had nothing to do with people with disabilities who use it. In fact, I fully respect that people have the right to describe themselves using the language that feels correct to them. Instead, I was tired of mostly nondisabled people telling me that PFL was right and IFL was wrong. I was tired of calling myself "disabled" and being told "oh, you shouldn't talk about yourself like that," or "I don't even think of you as disabled." Certainly, there are people with disabilities who prefer not to be identified by their disabilities, but in my case, hearing such things makes me feel as if a whole facet of my existence is simply being erased. I know that people who say these kinds of things mean well, but it doesn't feel so great to know that the only way some people can conceive of the fact that I'm a human being is to downplay or ignore a significant part of that being. So I'm still partial to IFL. But with the realization that I didn't like being told what to call myself came an understanding that I couldn't tell other people what to call themselves.

There are no right or wrong personal choices about IFL and PFL. But there *are* some important things to consider about using them respectfully. Many people with intellectual and developmental disabilities intentionally use PFL, as it is historically rooted in what is known as the People First movement, which emphasizes that people with disabilities are, first and foremost, people. It is a language-based reminder that people with disabilities deserve to have their humanity fully recognized, just like everyone else. Within the Autistic community, however, IFL is preferred and often consciously chosen by many people who count Autism as part of their identity. So you'd say "Autistic person" instead of "person with Autism." Notice the capital "A"? That's often used as a way of showing that Autistic people are part of a broader culture and community. (For the sake of simplicity, I chose to use the capital "A" throughout this book unless quoting someone who used a lowercase "a.") In a 2011 blog post on Autistic Hoya, Autistic activist Lydia X. Z. Brown elaborates:

> These are not qualities or conditions that I have. They are part of who I am. Being Autistic does not subtract from my value, worth, and dignity as a person. Being Autistic does not diminish the other aspects of my identity. Being Autistic is not giving up on myself or limiting myself or surrendering to some debilitating monster or putting myself down. Being Autistic is like being anything else.

This same line of thinking is followed by lots of people who are deaf or blind. While many identify as deaf or blind (with the lowercase "d" or "b" referring to a physical state of being), others use these terms as indicators of a cultural identity. In some cases, people capitalize the "D" or "B" to indicate this identity. And sometimes, people will identify as d/Deaf, b/Blind, or d/Deafblind (written this way to show respect for both ways of identifying), but not as disabled. (Again, for the sake of simplicity, I use the lowercase "d" and "b," unless I'm quoting someone who prefers it to be capitalized.) Jenny Lay-Flurrie, chief accessibility officer of Microsoft, shared with me that she identifies as both, stating, "Disability is a part of being human. It's a part of me. I grew up with declining hearing and am now profoundly deaf. I'm proud to be a member of the deaf and hard of hearing community, and learn from my friends daily. It's a label that assists but does not define me or anyone else. My name is Jenny, and I happen to be deaf."

Still with me? Great! Here's where things can get a little tricky and the rules change. When it comes to certain diagnoses, using them in the format of IFL is not appropriate. For example, you shouldn't call someone a "Down syndrome person" or "muscular dystrophy person." But if someone's okay with it, you could say "bipolar person" or "dyslexic person." Don't worry if this seems confusing. One of the simplest ways to avoid incorrectly using IFL is to default to PFL until and unless you're informed otherwise. If you have the opportunity to ask what someone prefers, then ask! If not, go ahead and say "person with dyslexia." If you happen to be speaking with someone who has dyslexia and they tell you they prefer "dyslexic person," use that instead.

There is one form of address that's off limits all the time, *always*. Please do not ever refer to someone by their mobility equipment. Not only is this rude but to equate a person to an object completely undermines one's humanity. If you're trying to find an easy way to identify a specific person, you might be inclined to describe someone as "the cane guy" or "the hearing-aid lady." But it's just as straightforward to say, "the guy who uses a cane" or "the lady who wears hearing aids." As for me, I've been called "the wheelchair" so many times, as in "Watch out for the wheelchair" or "I have to load the wheelchair onto the bus." And once, as I entered a building, a security guard started yelling "Wheelchair person! Hey! Wheelchair person!" to get my attention. "Wheelchair person" is *not* IFL. Instead, say "wheelchair user" or "person who uses a wheelchair." A person is a person, not a piece of equipment.

And since we're on the subject of mobility equipment, allow me to share my biggest language pet peeve: the terms "con-fined to a wheelchair" and "wheelchair-bound." I can't tell you how many articles I read that have otherwise good points about disability but then refer to wheelchair users as *confined* to their mobility equipment. I'm not confined or bound to my wheelchair. It's literally designed to enable me to move.

Phew! If this feels like a lot to take in, that's okay. It's totally normal to worry that you'll mess up on what to say, even if you're trying your best. And if you get it wrong, just apologize, move on, and try to do better in the future. There's no need to dwell on it by apologizing multiple times or to make it about you by going on about how embarrassed you are. You'll get the hang of it.

Just Say It: "Disability"

By now, you can probably tell I'm not one to sugarcoat things. So you can imagine I might get a little salty when people use euphemisms (terms used to soften something deemed unpleasant, harsh, or offensive) for *disabled* or *disability*. You've definitely heard examples of these before—terms such as *physically challenged* or *special needs*. Maybe you've even said them in an attempt to be respectful. But have you ever asked yourself why? Is it because you've been taught that the term *disabled* is rude or wrong? Does the word *disability* make you uncomfortable?

I get it. We've been socialized to think of disability as a negative thing, so your instinct might be to sidestep the word. Personally, I'd rather you say what you actually mean. And that's not just my preference. For so many disabled people, it would be a relief if everyone would just start being straightforward. After all, avoiding the use of *disabled* to refer to me won't make me any less so. Neither will changing the way the word is written to *disAbled* or *disAbility*, as I've seen many people do in an attempt to downplay the actual meaning.

That being said, as with PFL and IFL, it's all about choice. For example, Kayla McKeon, a powerhouse advocate who has Down syndrome, calls herself "differently abled." "I like to say differently abled," she told me, "because I like focusing on what I can do rather than what I can't do." Though I prefer to call myself disabled, I respect McKeon's choice and make sure to use it when referring to her. But what really gets to me are non-disabled people making up their own ways to dance around disability. "Diff-ability"? "Other-abled"? "People of special

Don't Dance Around "Disability"

While euphemisms for disability are generally intended to be well-meaning, they usually fall flat. Here are the most common ones.

Differently abled

No two people are able to do exactly the same things in exactly the same ways. Some people can sing. Some people can solve a Rubik's cube in sixty seconds. Some people can cook. Some people can contort like a pretzel. Technically, disabled people aren't the only ones who are differently abled. We all are.

Handi-capable

Does anyone seriously use this? Please don't.

Mentally or physically challenged

It's true that certain things are more difficult for people who have disabilities, but so many of our challenges are caused by things beyond our control. After all, stigmatizing attitudes, places that we can't access, and laws that don't protect our rights are all challenges, but they're not the fault of disabled people.

Special needs

It is the most universally human thing to have needs, so I've never understood how having a disability translates to having "special needs." No one has their needs met in exactly the same way.

Twice exceptional

Parents and teachers of students with disabilities often use this term to reconcile the fact that a student with a learning disability can also be considered "gifted" in certain subject areas. But it's not *exceptional* to be good at some things and struggle with others; it's *human*.

abilities"? I've heard them all. I wish people would stop doing this and just call me what I am.

So whenever possible, ask people to share their preferred terminology. It's as easy as saying, "Would it be okay to say that you're disabled, or is there another term you prefer?" But if the opportunity to ask doesn't come up and you're unsure about a person's preference, go ahead and say "disabled." It's perfectly okay and not a bad word, I promise!

Normal Human Function Doesn't Exist

I have a question for you. What does "normal" mean? Sure, you could Google the definition, but can you actually envision one single person who embodies that definition in looks, behavior, or abilities? If you answered yes, please think again. Our bodies and brains work in different ways. We process things differently; we communicate things differently; we move differently. This means we all need help and support in different ways to get things done. Yet far too many of us are hung up on categorizing people based on some arbitrary idea of normalcy, which is where *functioning labels* come into play.

Often, especially in medical or school settings, disabled people are referred to as *high functioning* or *low functioning*. For example, I've been called "high functioning" because my disability doesn't affect my ability to write or speak. Placing this label on me isn't a compliment. It wrongly pits me against people whose disabilities impact their writing and speaking abilities, holding me up as somehow superior to them. Noor Pervez, an Autistic activist, further explained to me why functioning labels are both inaccurate and harmful. "'Low functioning' is used to deny agency to disabled people who have high support needs," he states, "while 'high functioning' is used to deny resources to people who can mask their disability well. Any person's support needs can shift from year to year, or even day to day, making 'functioning' a flawed concept."

I hereby move to strike these terms from use entirely, because they're based on a "normal" standard of function that just doesn't exist. Functioning labels promote the false idea that there are standard abilities that *all* people have. There's no need to create this kind of divide between nondisabled people and disabled people, or between people who have different disabilities, because everyone functions differently. Instead, it's better to speak openly and directly about needs, abilities, and disabilities. Consider a conversation between a parent of a young child with a disability and the child's teacher. Rather than referring to the student as "low functioning" in math, the teacher can say, "I've noticed your child needs more support in completing his math assignments" or "Your child might benefit from extra support to complete her math homework." Such language is simple, straightforward, and respectful without placing a harmful label on the student.

Think Before You Speak

There's a pretty good chance that almost all of us have, at some point, blurted out "That's *insane!*" in the middle of an enthusiastic conversation. Or you've been driving down the road, minding your own business, and someone cuts you off, prompting you to mutter, "Ugh, *moron.*" Maybe you got a bit of disappointing news and found yourself thinking, "This is so *lame.*" It might seem as though you're harmlessly expressing your thoughts and feelings, but if you're doing that using such words, unfortunately, you're being ableist (a concept we'll dive into deeper in chapter 4) by perpetuating the idea that disability is a negative thing. Words have histories connected to stigmatizing disability. Some were once considered acceptable terms, and others have always had derogatory connotations.

These words are so embedded in our language that it takes active practice and a conscious effort to break away from using them. I've been guilty of saying some of them, but I often don't catch myself until the word is already out of my mouth and then I can't take it back. What I can do—what we can all do—is try to do better next time, until we've eliminated the words from our vocabulary. Some of the most common examples to look out for include *crazy, dumb, idiot, imbecile, insane, lame, moron, slow,* and *stupid*. Words such as these were historically used to refer to people with disabilities, often as official diagnoses for people who were housed in institutions. Practice removing these terms from your vocabulary. Not only are they outdated; they're hurtful and offensive. And there are plenty of alternatives.

In addition to everyday words rooted in disability stigma, many phrases that rely on disability to explain feelings or circumstances have infiltrated the English language. You've probably heard plenty of these. Imagine this conversation:

"He's obviously *paralyzed* by fear of rejection."

"No way! He's totally using that excuse as a *crutch* not to ask for her number."

"Well, she's clearly *blind* to his crush on her."

"Seems like his attempts to get her attention fell on *deaf* ears."

It's easy to fall back on using disability as a metaphor, but it's just as easy to avoid. Here's the same conversation without any mentions of disability:

"He's obviously *frozen* by fear of rejection."

"No way! He's totally *leaning on that* as an excuse not to ask for her number."

"Well, she's clearly *oblivious* to his crush on her."

"Seems like she *isn't noticing* his attempts to get her attention."

See? All it takes are simple changes.

Find a Better Insult

Disability is not an insult. I cannot stress this enough. *Do not* use disability as an insult. I constantly notice people saying things such as:

- She's so bipolar.
- They're acting Autistic.
- Quit being so OCD.

These are cheap shots that use actual diagnoses to be derogatory, and that's just not okay. When we use disabilities in this negative way, we're perpetuating harmful stereotypes. So if you really must say something insulting (though it'd be better if we were all just a little bit more kind to one another), please find other words.

Drop These Words

There are some words that aren't just insults; they're outright slurs. Let's talk about some of the most egregious examples. "Retarded" (otherwise known as the "R-word") is incredibly hurtful to people with intellectual disabilities, and yet there are people who still throw it around like it means nothing. Once, while on a date, the guy I was with paused to look me in the eyes and said, "I'm so retardedly attracted to you." Instant mood killer, to say the very least, and obviously I did not go out with him again. But the moment stuck with me, because it was a stark reminder of just how ignorant some people can be to the pain that such slurs cause.

Then there's the word "midget" (otherwise known as the "M-word"), a slur against people with dwarfism. Unfortunately it's so culturally pervasive that a few towns have actually used it as a team mascot. Please don't be like those towns. Instead, say "little person," "person with dwarfism," or "short-statured." As Rebecca Cokley, program officer for the U.S. Disability Rights portfolio at the Ford Foundation and life member of the organization Little People of America, explained to me, the M-word is derived from *midge*, a term used to refer to fruit flies. "It was co-opted and commodified by the carnival, sideshow, and circus industry to describe people with various types of dwarfism," she says. "It was a word used to sell us as a product to a curious public. It is not a word we, as a community, ever chose for ourselves."

Then there are words such as "cripple," "gimp," and "spaz," all of which are slurs against physically disabled people. And words such as "mad" and "crazy," which are slurs against people with mental illness. But here's where it gets interesting. Many disabled people actually choose to reclaim these words to take back power. My mom and I call ourselves "cripples" all the time, tossing it back and forth as we lament our various bodily aches and pains or joke about silly disability-related mishaps. Sometimes, people who are very close to us might join in and joke around. That said, it's absolutely not appropriate for nondisabled people to use the word "crippled" as a general term instead of "disabled." It's *only* okay to use it to refer to a specific disabled person if you have their express permission. And it's never okay for anyone, disabled or not, to push the use of such words on other disabled people. The best policy if you're not sure whether a word is offensive or a slur is always to choose a different word.

What to Say

Remember, it's always best to ask a person what terms work for them based on their own lived experiences and identity. We'll unpack some of the words and concepts from this table throughout the book.

Say This	Not This
✓ disability/disabled ✓ person with a disability/ disabled person	✗ differently abled (unless preferred) ✗ handi-capable ✗ handicap/handicapped ✗ special needs (unless preferred)
✓ has a disability ✓ is disabled	✗ afflicted by ✗ suffers from ✗ victim of
✓ person who is able to	✗ high functioning
✓ person who is unable to ✓ person with high support needs	✗ low functioning

Say This	Not This
✓ neurodivergent°	✗ mentally challenged
✓ person with Autism/ Autistic person°	✗ mentally handicapped
✓ person with a cognitive disability/cognitively disabled person°	✗ mentally retarded
✓ person with an intellectual disability/ intellectually disabled person°	✗ slow
✓ person with a learning disability/learning disabled person°	✗ special-ed

Say This	Not This
✓ able-bodied (if not physically disabled)	✗ normal
✓ does not have a disability	✗ regular
✓ neurotypical (if not neurodivergent)	
✓ nondisabled	

° These types of disabilities are not all the same but are often grouped together.

continued →

Say This	Not This
✓ person who uses a wheelchair	× wheelchair-bound
✓ wheelchair user	× confined to a wheelchair
✓ little person	× midget
✓ person of short stature	
✓ person with dwarfism/ dwarf	
✓ person with a mental health disability	× crazy*
✓ person with mental illness/mentally ill person	× disturbed*
✓ person with a psychiatric disability/ psychiatrically disabled person	× insane*
	× lunatic*
	× mad*
	× psychotic*

Say This	Not This
✓ person with a physical disability/physically disabled person	× cripple*
	× gimp*
	× invalid*
	× spaz*
✓ accessible parking/ restroom	× disabled restroom
	× handicapped parking

* People may choose to reclaim these words as personal identifiers, but they should be used in reference to a person only with explicit permission.

Chapter 2

Understanding Disability as Part of a Whole Person

Disability must be considered within an intersectional framework because it cuts across political, social, and cultural narratives and identities. An intersectional lens challenges the historically white, cisgender, heterosexual understanding of disability to more accurately reflect the narratives as told by lived experiences of disabled people.

— Sandy Ho, community organizer

My relationship status with disability is complicated. On one hand, my disability is an integral facet of my being. It is completely intertwined with how I think and how I move. I consider it to be an identity—in many ways, my defining identity, although I don't want to be solely defined by it. Confusing, I know. I take pride in being disabled, and it's brought me to a whole culture and community that I love. But on the other hand, it's not always sunshine and roses. I struggle with physical pain every day. I feel the emotional toll from lack of acceptance, sometimes from others, sometimes within myself. But I am disabled. It's part of me.

Here's some food for thought: Disability is the only identity that anyone can suddenly take on at any time. Don't worry, though! That's not a threat. Disabled people are actually pretty cool, in my humble opinion. Disability is deeply personal and means different things to different people. Some people consider disability to be an identity. Some consider it part of who they are, but not an identity. And some who technically have disabilities choose not to identify as disabled at all. This choice is based on any number of factors and is totally up to each individual person.

Let's think of disability identity as a pizza. The crust is the foundation of who you are—your actual being. While every pizza has a crust, it's the toppings that make each individual pizza what it is. There can be infinite combinations of toppings. And even though millions of pizzas are made with the same toppings, no two slices are exactly alike. Having or not having a disability might seem like the most straightforward of the factors that influence what disability means to a person, but it's actually not quite that simple. Not only does everything on the following list influence what "disability" means to someone, but each factor also determines whether a person chooses to identify as having a disability—or reveals their disability at all. What toppings might be on a person's metaphorical pizza?

- Having or not having a disability
- The type of disability they have
- Whether they're born with a disability or acquire one later in life
- Whether their disability is visible or invisible (More on this on page 37!)
- Where they live
- The environment around them at any given time (Are they home? In a safe space? Somewhere surrounded by new people?)
- How people around them perceive disability
- How their culture as a whole perceives disability
- How their other identities intersect with disability

Intersectionality: It's Not Just a Buzzword

Coined in 1989 by Dr. Kimberlé Crenshaw, the term *intersectionality* was originally used to describe the experience of Black womanhood. Being Black and female are both separate aspects of identity, Dr. Crenshaw explained, but neither can be considered in isolation. In other words, every identity that a person has will intersect to make them who they are.

These days, the concept of intersectionality has become a central tenet of social justice activism. It's a term that should not be thrown around lightly, though, without understanding why you're using it. In the context of disability, it's particularly important to think about because *disability can intersect with any and all other identities*. And when we say "intersectionality," we have to recognize that it's about centering the lived experiences of marginalized people whose multiple identities overlap.

The other identities that people have in addition to disability can impact both how they experience disability and how people perceive and treat them. I'm a disabled, straight, white, Jewish, cisgender woman (meaning I identify as the gender that I was assigned at birth), so the ways I experience life are definitely different from the experiences of disabled people who are, to name just a few examples, Black, or transgender, or Muslim, or Indigenous. I'm actually what many people might envision when they consider disability at surface level: a white, cisgender, wheelchair-using woman. I fall right in line with the little white symbol on a blue background that you see on parking signs and bathroom stalls.

This is where my privilege, a concept strongly tied to intersectionality, comes into play. *Privilege* refers to advantages some people have in comparison to others because of identities that they do or do not have. Nondisabled people certainly have privilege in ways that disabled people do not. Think about employment. Disabled people (especially people with disabilities that are noticeable) are much more likely to experience discrimination and other barriers to finding a job. According to the U.S. Bureau of Labor Statistics, in 2019, the employment-to-population ratio—the proportion of the population that is employed—was 19.3 percent for disabled people, as compared to 66.3 percent for nondisabled people. These numbers are a prime example of nondisabled privilege.

But keep in mind that disabled people aren't exempt from experiencing privilege simply because they're disabled. As a white disabled person, I am afforded privilege that people of color (both disabled and nondisabled) are not. And because my disability doesn't impact my ability to communicate verbally, I experience privilege not shared with people who don't communicate verbally. Privilege and lack thereof take many forms, and we can't talk about disability without constantly acknowledging that humans are complex, with overlapping, intersecting identities and opportunities that influence how we perceive the world and how the world perceives us. In a 2016 *Time* magazine article, filmmaker and writer Crystal R. Emery makes these connections clear:

> As an African American female with a disability, a wheelchair-riding quadriplegic, I exist as a triple threat to our society's normative conceptions (white, male, able-bodied). . . . My gender, race, and disability all contribute to the ways in which I obtain and maintain power—not through my intersectional identity but through my search to become human in ways not easily codified. In spite of my reimagined relationship with these identity markers, the world has a lot to catch up on.

So how can we do the necessary catching up? How can we unlearn and disentangle ourselves from the mess of stigma and prejudice toward disabled people—especially disabled people of multiple marginalized identities—and begin to move toward a more inclusive, accepting world? We have a long way to go, but we can and should focus on doing the work of examining our own biases and privileges. This work is necessary for both nondisabled people and disabled people because, as doctoral student D'Arcee Neal rightly pointed out to me, "being part of one marginalized community doesn't absolve you from understanding discrimination toward marginalized people whose experiences are different than your own." Noting that he can speak only to this broader concept in relation to his experience as a Black, queer, physically disabled man, Neal shared some concrete, hard-hitting examples of his experiences as a person who exists at the intersection of multiple marginalized identities. "People need to recognize that being Black means you're perceived as being criminal, whether you have a disability or not," he says. "When I tell people I have cerebral palsy, they're surprised because that's not the first association they made with why I'm a wheelchair user. When I was younger, the very first question most white people would ask upon meeting me was 'When were you shot?' They immediately jumped to the conclusion that I had a spinal cord injury as a result of gang or gun violence."

Neal emphasized that this particular experience stemmed from specific stereotypes associated with people who look like him. Taking into account all three of his marginalized identities, some-one once told him, "I would kill myself if I were you." (Side note: Please do not say this to any disabled person, *ever*.) "He told me that my life is too difficult," Neal said. This person, whom Neal has never spoken to again, made a value judgment about his own life based on his biases toward Neal's identities. And the thing is, Neal does experience difficulties, but not because of who he is. They're because of who society determines him to be, based on prejudice.

The experiences that Neal recalled shed light on just how crucial it is to recognize that disability experiences are *not* all the same. Bias and privilege are deeply linked to our understanding of identity—our own and others'—and we must keep this front and center in our minds as we dig deeper into ideas and concepts connected to disability.

Types of Disabilities

There are so many kinds of disabilities that I could fill the rest of this book just listing them. Instead of focusing on individual names of disabilities or diagnoses, let's break it down into a broader overview of the most commonly recognized types. Keep in mind that many disabilities, like Autism or cerebral palsy, don't fit neatly into one category. Disabilities can coexist within a person. In my case, I have hearing, mental health, and physical disabilities. The following are generally recognized broad categories of disabilities, but each exists in infinite different forms.

- **Chronic illnesses** can have an ongoing effect on varying aspects of a person's physical and mental health.
- **Communication disorders** affect how a person conveys and/ or comprehends information.
- **Developmental disabilities** can affect the trajectory of a person's physical or cognitive growth.

- **Hearing disabilities** partially or completely affect a person's ability to hear.
- **Intellectual disabilities** can affect a person's communication, cognition, and personal and interpersonal activities.
- **Learning disabilities** affect the ways a person can learn, process, and understand different subject areas.
- **Mental health disabilities** can affect a person's thoughts, moods, and behavior.
- **Neurological disorders** can affect different parts of a person's nervous system, which can in turn affect them in many ways, including physically, cognitively, and emotionally.
- **Physical disabilities** can affect a person's movement, dexterity, or stamina.
- **Vision disabilities** partially or completely affect a person's ability to see.

You can find more information about specific disabilities in Further Reading and Resources on page 150.

Apparent and Nonapparent Disabilities

Based on the way disability is portrayed in the media (which we'll talk about more in chapter 6), it can be easy to fall into the assumption that disabled people look a certain way. But that's just not the case. While many disabilities do have specific physical features associated with them, it's important not to make assumptions about a person's disability status based solely on how they look, especially because not all disabilities are apparent.

An **apparent** or **visible disability** is one that's noticeable to other people based on either outward appearance or communication. So you might see someone who has physical features that are different from yours. Maybe you'll pass by a person walking with an uneven gait. Someone could be rolling in a wheelchair or walking while holding a white cane in front of them. You might notice that a person has a limb difference and is wearing an artificial arm or leg (called a prosthetic). Or your could strike up a conversation with someone and hear that they have a stutter. All of these are examples of apparent disabilities.

A **nonapparent** or **invisible disability** is something you likely can't tell a person has when looking at or communicating with them. Often, this means you won't even know a person has a nonapparent disability unless they tell you (which is *their* decision). It may be possible for people with invisible disabilities to "pass" as nondisabled, meaning that they're assumed not to be disabled because there are no outwardly visible or otherwise noticeable signs. So, for example, you might not be aware of someone's learning disability or mental illness. And there are many physical disabilities, such as chronic pain, that can't be observed just by looking at a person.

Additionally, the same disability can be apparent at certain times and invisible at others, depending on any number of circumstances both within and outside a person's body. For instance, if you're communicating with me or my mom face to face in a quiet environment, you likely won't notice that we have hearing loss. But if we're trying to have a conversation in a loud restaurant, there's a good chance you'll be able to tell that we're not quite able to hear what you're saying.

One type of disability is no more or less valid than any other type. Just because my disability is visible doesn't make it more legitimate than a disability that's nonapparent. And no disability makes anyone more or less of a whole person. Someone whose disability manifests in ways that impact them more severely than mine impacts me, for example, should never be regarded as less of a person.

There are also **temporary disabilities**, such as broken bones, and **acquired disabilities**, like hearing loss, paralysis, and brain injuries. In fact, some people with disabilities like to refer to non-disabled people as **temporarily able-bodied**, meaning that disability is something we'll most likely all experience at some point in our lives.

To most nondisabled people, the idea of becoming disabled is pretty scary. I get it. It's natural to fear the unknown, and it's tough to grapple with the idea that our bodies can change in ways beyond our control. Unfortunately, these fears often translate to stigma against disabled people, because it can be challenging to accept that another person's reality may become one's own. This is why we need to have open, honest conversations about disability. We need to reframe these fears and turn them into an understanding of disability as part of the human experience.

Choose Your Model

There are lots of frameworks—often referred to as models—that we can use to understand disability. It might sound as if we're about to get academic here, but I promise this is pretty simple. Models are ways to conceptualize disability as it relates to who we are and the world around us. To have a full picture, it's important to think about how the models of disability overlap. Let's start with the two most common modes of thinking about disability: the medical model and the social model.

The **medical model**, also known as the "individual model," focuses on disability as a person-based issue. It's about defining disability as a diagnosis or impairment that has an effect on an individual. There's definitely merit to this model. The fact that I have Larsen syndrome is absolutely relevant to who I am and how I move about the world. It causes low muscle function and joint dislocations, which limit or prevent me from doing certain things. It also causes chronic pain, which can be understood as a medical issue. That said, there are some big downfalls to the medical model; namely, the negative attitudes toward disability that it frequently perpetuates and the idea that disability is a problem needing to be fixed or cured. It also ignores the fact that the effects of disability aren't limited to just a person's body.

The **social model** emerged as a response to the incomplete perspective of the medical model. According to the social model, people are disabled not by medical conditions but by environments, attitudes, and systems that create barriers. As an example, through the lens of the social model, I can attribute my status as disabled to an environment that isn't wheelchair accessible, rather than to my medical diagnosis.

In reality, neither the medical nor the social model can exist independently of each other. The ways that I experience my disability can be different from moment to moment. Sometimes I'll try to reach something I dropped on the floor and complain loudly while I struggle to pick it up, or I'll wake up to a chronic pain flare and dramatically whine about how "I feel *soooo* disabled right now." In those instances, my perception of disability is based on my impairment and physical experiences.

But when I encounter a restaurant that people can enter only by using steps, or a person who makes a rude comment about my wheelchair, my physical limitations or sensations aren't the issue. Instead, it's attitudes and obstacles beyond my control that are disabling.

Other Models of Disability

Of course, we can go further than the medical and social models. There are lots of other ways to think about and explain disability. Here are just a few.

- **Charity model** From this perspective, disability is a tragedy that warrants pity. Far too many nondisabled people think that disabled people are tragic souls in need of good deeds, as though we're victims of our circumstances. And if we "over-come" those circumstances, we're suddenly front and center in an inspirational story on the six o'clock news. The thing is, disabled people do need support, but not in the form of warm, fuzzy feelings. We need support to access resources, to embrace ourselves without shame, and to live full lives.
- **Cultural model** By centering on disability as a culture with a rich history and shared identity among disabled people, this model embraces the experience of disability and how it shapes people.

- **Economic model** This viewpoint considers disability from the perspective of productivity—or rather, the impact that disability has on productivity. It essentially attributes a person's worth to their contribution to the economy at large and the ability to provide for their household. In this model, those whose disabilities render them unable to hold a job are commonly perceived as burdens on society.

- **Human rights model** In this context, disability is viewed as a human rights issue. It's about taking into account the social factors that impact disabled people and about writing inclusion and equality into the law.

- **Religious model** This is a tale as old as time—or at least as old as religion. Through this model, disability is seen as a curse, a punishment for a sin, or, on the flip side, a special blessing bestowed on only those who can "handle" it. I've encountered people who believe I can be "healed" if only I pray for it. Or they'll pray over me, usually without asking first (see page 106). Not cool.

While various models offer ways to wrap our minds around disability, none of them fully encapsulates the depth and breadth of disability. And unfortunately, some of these models—specifically the charity, economic, and religious—are based on perceptions of disability that are quite inaccurate and harmful. Each of these models is helpful in explaining the ways that our society perceives and understands disability; but ultimately, disability is a complex human experience that can't be placed squarely into any one category.

Chapter 3

An (Incomplete) Overview of Disability History

As "invisibles," our history is hidden from us, our heroes buried in the pages, unnamed, unrecognized. Disability culture is about naming, about recognizing.

— Cheryl Marie Wade, "Disability Culture Rap"

Think about the history lessons you've learned. Whether they're fresh in your mind or feel like forever ago, there's one thing I can assume about them with relative certainty: Disability didn't come up much, if at all. Neither disability-specific history nor discussion about how disability is part of history in a larger context were topics that came up during my school days. Did you know that abolitionist and Underground Railroad "conductor" Harriet Tubman was disabled? A slave owner threw a weight at her that caused head trauma, leading to a form of epilepsy. Did you know that artist Frida Kahlo acquired physical disabilities from both polio and a bus accident? And did you know that President Franklin Delano Roosevelt (FDR) contracted polio at age thirty-nine and, as a result, was paralyzed from the waist down and used mobility aids, including a wheelchair, to get around? These are all recognizable names, but when you look back on their legacies, I bet disability was nowhere near the first thing to come to mind.

And do you know of Justin Dart Jr. and Yoshiko Dart? Bradley Lomax? Anita Cameron? Lois Curtis? If you're thinking *who?*, that's okay. We'll fix that in this section, but know that you're not alone.

In fact, it wasn't until 2006 in West Virginia that a group of young disabled advocates finally succeeded in pushing for state legislation that requires all public schools to teach students about the history of disability. So far, only a handful of other states have since followed suit.

But before you start getting textbook vibes and abandon me for a juicy beach read, allow me to reassure you again that this isn't that kind of book. My goal isn't to put you to sleep; it's to invite you to feel the rhythmic drumbeat of movement toward disability rights and autonomy—a goal that is nowhere near fully realized today, although we *are* closer to reaching it. The history of disability isn't a separate, isolated thread of human existence. It is a saga that encompasses all people and places and is deeply intertwined with who we were, are, and will become. Yet it's still considered a niche area of study rather than necessary to understanding what shapes our society.

The disability community has quite the storied past, ranging from painful oppression to hard-won civil rights victories. We can trace records of disability all the way back to ancient Sparta, where disabled infants were left to die because they were deemed worthless if they couldn't be warriors. We can trace support of disabled veterans back to the 1600s, when the Pilgrims enacted a law declaring that soldiers defending Plymouth would be supported by the colony if they became disabled. We can pull back the curtain on P. T. Barnum's freak shows, which he started in the 1800s as a way to make money by putting people with physical differences on display for the gawking public's pleasure. There are thousands of years to unpack, but let's leave those deep dives to professional historians.

I'll be limiting my overview to United States–based events that occurred from the early twentieth century onward and that I believe have directly impacted the rights and freedoms that I personally enjoy, as well as the prejudice and discrimination I still experience. This is by no means a comprehensive overview of disability history. Rather, these moments in time resonate deeply with me as a disabled person, and I hope they'll pique your interest to learn more. And remember, there's no pop quiz at the end of this section.

The Turn of the Twentieth Century

As much as I'd prefer starting on a high note, the early 1900s wasn't an easy time for disabled people. There was widespread belief that disability was a flaw in humanity and needed to be eradicated, and this dogma was written into laws across the country. In 1907, Indiana's state legislature passed an ordinance known to be the first of its kind, calling for involuntary sterilization of "confirmed criminals, idiots, imbeciles, and rapists." This dangerous practice is known as eugenics—a set of beliefs and practices intended to prevent people with "undesirable" traits from reproducing for the supposed betterment of humankind. And who got to decide who qualified as "desirable"? Nondisabled, white, straight, cisgender people.

As if Indiana's law wasn't horrifying enough, more than half of the United States followed suit. By 1927, a legal battle over eugenics came to a head. A teenager named Carrie Buck was institutionalized at the Virginia State Colony for Epileptics and Feebleminded. The justification? She was poor and uneducated, and she had given birth to a child out of wedlock, just like her mother, Emma. While Buck was in the institution, doctors cruelly determined that these three characteristics were reason enough for her to be forcibly sterilized so she wouldn't be able to have any more children. The matter was escalated all the way to the U.S. Supreme Court, which ruled that forced sterilization was not a violation of the Constitution. In his haunting opinion on the case, Justice Oliver Wendell Holmes Jr. declared, "Three generations of imbeciles are enough."

The 1930s: Disability and the Great Depression

Even as the eugenic mindset kept its hold on the nation, a privileged few disabled people found success. One of them was FDR, who was elected in 1932 and remains the only man with a significant visible physical disability to serve as a U.S. president. For the most part, he was able to hide his disability from the public—no small feat considering the public nature of his role. He believed this secrecy was a necessity, though, fearing that widespread knowledge of his disability would detract from his authority.

These days, knowledge of FDR's disability is considerably more common. And after much controversy, a memorial in Washington, DC, now includes a statue of him seated in a wheelchair. But at the time, FDR's success was an anomaly for disabled people. Finding work during the Great Depression was already an immense challenge; but for people with disabilities, it was nearly impossible. In 1935, a group of disabled people, fed up with this barrier, gathered to protest the discrimination they encountered from the Works Progress Administration and other agencies that were meant to help them find jobs. This gathering was the official formation of the League of the Physically Handicapped, one of the earliest known organized disability rights groups.

Shortly thereafter, the Social Security Act of 1935 was passed, establishing a financial safety net that included support for "crippled children," as well as funding for vocational rehabilitation (VR) for people with disabilities—services to support them in finding and keeping employment. VR includes a range of services meant to help disabled people begin or return to a job. Three years later, Congress passed the Fair Labor Standards Act of 1938. As part of an effort to create job opportunities for disabled people—mainly wounded veterans—the law included a provision enabling employers to apply for certificates from the U.S. Department of Labor granting them special permission to pay workers with disabilities (most often intellectual or developmental disabilities) significantly below minimum wage. And by "significantly below," I mean mere pennies per hour. Though supposedly well-intentioned, as of this writing, the law is still in place, which means that wage discrimination on the basis of disability is still legal.

The 1940s: World War II and Its Aftermath

In the first half of the 1940s, America's economy regained its equilibrium, thanks chiefly to job creation as World War II raged. But disabled people largely continued to encounter societal barriers. In 1943, the Disabled Veterans Rehabilitation Act went into effect to help wounded veterans find employment. And after the war finally concluded in 1945, Congress established that the first week of every October would be designated "National Employ the Physically Handicapped Week." President Harry S. Truman issued a proclamation urging employers in every sector "to exercise every appropriate effort to enlist public support of a sustained program for the employment and development of the abilities and capacities of those who are physically handicapped." By 1988, a series of legislative actions would change the observance into the much more inclusively named "National Disability Employment Awareness Month." It's now observed each October to honor the skills and talents that people with all types of disabilities bring to the workforce.

Organizing among groups of disabled people gained momentum throughout the decade. Beginning in 1940, blind people from around the country joined together to found the National Federation of the Blind. They were the first, and now largest, national advocacy organization for blind people. In 1946, veterans who returned home from World War II with spinal cord injuries joined together to form Paralyzed Veterans of America (PVA), an organization centered on advocacy for the rights of disabled veterans and other quality-of-life issues.

Physical disabilities weren't the only focus of the time, though. In the wake of the war, as staggering numbers of veterans grappled with the traumatic aftereffects of combat (known then as "combat fatigue"), came the start of a much-needed shift in public consciousness around mental health. This strongly influenced the passage of the National Mental Health Act of 1946, which contributed to early stages of progress in mental health care reform. The law was key to beginning the slow (and still far from complete) move away from placing people with mental illness in institutions for treatment.

The 1950s: Advancements in Social Security

It wasn't until the middle of the twentieth century that amendments to Social Security and vocational rehabilitation laws expanded financial protections and employment support for people with disabilities. In 1954, President Dwight D. Eisenhower signed amendments that increased the available funding for VR and ensured that previously employed people who were unable to work because of a disability wouldn't be at risk of losing their Social Security benefits. Following this, in 1956, further amendments to the Social Security Act established Social Security Disability Insurance (SSDI). Today, SSDI provides monthly cash benefits to people who are unable to work for a year or more because of a disability that meets the Social Security Administration's guidelines. The larger goal of the legislation, though, is for people to return to work. Since its implementation, SSDI has been a hot-button issue for political debate, with conservatives making the ableist argument that it enables laziness, and progressives emphasizing that the program is a social and financial necessity.

The 1960s: Toward Access and Acceptance

The early 1960s saw a shift in mental health policy and the civil rights of people with intellectual and developmental disabilities, due in large part to the work of President John F. Kennedy's administration. In 1963, Kennedy signed the Mental Retardation and Community Mental Health Centers Construction Act. Dubbed the Community Mental Health Act (CMHA), this law established community mental health centers as much-needed alternatives to asylums.

The Kennedy family has continued this legacy. Kennedy's sister, Eunice Kennedy Shriver, launched the Special Olympics in 1968. The first international games were held in Chicago, and the program is still going strong today to break down the stigmas attached to people with intellectual and developmental disabilities. Loretta Claiborne, a multisport Special Olympics athlete with an intellectual disability, shared with me that she has found her experiences to be life-changing. As a result of being bullied, Claiborne often got in fights as a way to cope. Now, through her platform as a Special Olympian, she works hard to demonstrate what she can do, and she is helping to change attitudes toward people with disabilities.

Another big shift in policy also happened in 1968 with the passage of the Architectural Barriers Act, the first law on the books that mandated accessibility of buildings. Though it was focused only on buildings built with federal funds after the law's passage, it was a big push in the right direction for equal access.

The 1970s: The Fight for Rights Ramps Up

By the 1970s, the fight for disability rights was building toward a revolution. This action-packed decade began with a history-making lawsuit against the New York City Board of Education filed by disability rights activist Judith Heumann, then a twenty-two-year-old college graduate. While pursuing her teaching license, Heumann, who had contracted polio as a child and used a wheelchair, was met with discrimination during the required physical exam and denied her certification. As a budding, already fierce advocate, Heumann decided to fight back. And she won.

The year 1972 also saw news reporter Geraldo Rivera expose the repugnance of the Willowbrook State School in New York, an institution that warehoused disabled people. The horrors—people unclothed, unfed, living in complete filth (often in their own bodily waste)—had previously been unknown to the vast majority of the public. Despite Rivera's widely watched exposé, Willowbrook would continue to commit countless human rights violations, keeping residents trapped in absolutely vile conditions, right up until it finally closed in 1987. And although the effort to close asylums has gone on to this day, many disabled people remain in institutions instead of living in the community.

The Rehabilitation Act of 1973 came next. This landmark disability civil rights legislation addressed several key issues, including the formation of the U.S. Access Board to enforce and provide guidance on the Architectural Barriers Act, and the prohibition of discrimination on the basis of disability by federal programs, federally funded programs, and federal employers. In 1974 came the repeal of the last of what were known as the "Ugly Laws" in Chicago. Relics of the 1800s, such laws had existed around the United States to rid the streets of beggars who were deemed unfit for public view. These laws meant that people with visible physical differences could get in trouble simply for existing where others could see them, because they were deemed too unsightly.

Another milestone law, the Education for All Handicapped Children Act was passed in 1975 and established the right of all disabled kids to access public education. In 1997, this law was renamed the Individuals with Disabilities Education Act (IDEA). Although the IDEA has led to significant progress in education, it is not nearly enough, and despite having been in effect for decades, the implementation of the law has yet to be fully funded by the government (although the Biden/Harris administration has promised to change this).

As the disability community was making legislative gains in the 1970s, the urgency of the fight for their rights and independence remained. By 1977, regulations still hadn't been put in place to clearly define how the part of the Rehabilitation Act known as Section 504 should be legally interpreted. For the law to be adequately enforced, the Department of Health, Education, and Welfare (HEW) needed to provide clarification as to what constituted the broad concepts of "disability" and "discrimination." No big deal, right?

President Jimmy Carter's administration imposed lengthy delays on signing these regulations, and disability activists finally had enough. On April 5, 1977, sit-ins began at HEW offices around the country. No sit-in was quite as impactful as the one that occurred in the HEW building in San Francisco. It lasted nearly thirty days and still holds the record for the longest nonviolent occupation of a federal building in the United States. Known as the 504 Sit-In, this iconic protest brought together multiple social justice–conscious groups who worked in the community to push for action. Crucial to these efforts were the Black Panthers, including Bradley Lomax, a disabled member of the party who had already long been involved in disability rights work. The Black Panthers aided the sit-in through acts of support and solidarity, including bringing food to protestors inside the HEW building.

A group of the protestors—Lomax and Judith Heumann among them—traveled to Washington, DC, to garner more attention and force HEW Secretary Joseph Califano Jr. to sign the regulations.

Finally, on April 28, as a result of the tidal wave of powerful activism, Secretary Califano signed them. A hard-won victory for disability civil rights, with more to come. In Heumann's memoir, *Being Heumann*, she recalls the reaction to the protest: "The public was stunned. People weren't used to thinking of us as fighters—when they thought about us as all. . . . We were a people who were generally invisible in the daily life of society." The sit-in and the efforts of activists were key to helping to change that.

Around the country, grassroots activism efforts were continuing to take hold. In Denver, Colorado, a man named Wade Blank, who worked in the Heritage House nursing home, helped a group of nineteen young disabled people trapped there to free themselves and live with support in their community instead. This group, which became known as the "Gang of 19," led another seminal disability rights protest during the summer of 1978. The activists blocked an intersection—while chanting "We will ride!"—to force a meeting with local public transportation officials about the lack of wheelchair-accessible buses. This protest paved the way for future acts of civil disobedience to spark change.

The 1980s: Empowerment

Following the headline-worthy progress of the previous decade, the disability community continued to move full steam ahead. In 1983, the Gang of 19 officially formed what would become one of the most notable disability activist groups in the nation, American Disabled for Attendant Programs Today (ADAPT). Anita Cameron, a well-known Black disabled ADAPT activist, has been arrested more than 130 times for taking part in actions that involve nonviolent civil disobedience to fight for disability rights. In a 2018 interview with *Pacific Standard*, Cameron said, "If you're messing with our civil rights, you're going to hear from ADAPT."

In 1984, the Paralympic Games came to the United States for the first time. Started in 1948 as a sporting event for injured World War II veterans in Stoke Mandeville, England, the Games now take place during the same years as the Olympics, with disabled athletes from around the world competing.

Successes also continued on the political front, with two important pieces of legislation passing, both focused on ensuring access: the Voting Accessibility for the Elderly and Handicapped Act of 1984 and the Air Carrier Access Act of 1986. The first law mandated that polling places be accessible to disabled people, and the second mandated that commercial airlines can't discriminate against disabled people. While these were important (if small) steps forward, many disabled people—myself included—can personally attest to the fact that neither of these laws have been fully realized. While I'm not afraid of flying, I am scared of my wheelchair being broken in transit because it's stored in cargo and (mis)handled like luggage. And while I can exercise my right to vote because I'm able to access my polling place and mark a ballot, many disabled people still encounter barriers that exclude them from the process altogether. For example, people may be physically unable to get to polling places due to a lack of accessible transportation, or they may arrive only to find that poll workers are unable to operate the accessible voting machine for people with visual impairments.

As the 1980s came to a close, the fight for rights and representation continued. At Gallaudet University, a school for d/Deaf and hard of hearing people, an announcement that the board of trustees had appointed a hearing school president led students to launch a powerful protest, Deaf President Now (DPN). Greg Hlibok, then president of Gallaudet's student government, was one of the leaders of the protest efforts. Looking back and reflecting on the DPN movement as a turning point in efforts for disability representation, Hlibok shared with me that "It started as a campus issue where deaf individuals made their assertion known that a deaf person is fully capable of being a college president. It led to an explosion of awareness on accessibility and our language, American Sign Language, and created ripple effects that are part of a worldwide civil rights movement."

The 1990s: Civil Rights Victories

Disability rights activists brought in the 1990s with a bang. The groundbreaking Americans with Disabilities Act (ADA) was on the cusp of being signed into law, thanks to the hard work of disabled activists and the strong support of elected officials, including former senator Tom Harkin and the late congressman Major Owens. At the helm of the effort to push for its passage was Justin Dart Jr., an activist known as the father of the ADA. He and his wife, Yoshiko, along with other members of the disability community, went on a nationwide tour to speak with disabled people about the issues that mattered most to them and then used the information shared in these conversations while drafting the ADA. But as passage drew closer, the ADA hit a roadblock in the House of Representatives. Protestors joined together in March 1990 to galvanize legislators into action, among them a group of disabled people who left behind their mobility aids and hauled them-selves up the steps of the U.S. Capitol building to prove a point about the barriers they faced every day. Known as the "Capitol Crawl," it was one of the most iconic moments in the disabil-ity rights movement. In an interview in *New Mobility* magazine, ADAPT activist Anita Cameron, who took part in the Capitol Crawl, reflected, "I felt that we were crawling our way into the history books." Jennifer Keelan-Chaffins, who was just eight years old at the time, was among the protestors leading the way on the steps. "I'll take all night if I have to," she exclaimed while climbing. It's a moment I've watched on video so many times, and yet it still leaves me overcome with a sense of empowerment and pride. I had the opportunity to ask Keelan-Chaffins, founder of JKCLegacy.com and author of children's book *All the Way to the Top: How One Girl's Fight for Americans with Disabilities Changed Everything*, what that moment on the Capitol steps meant to her. "As a young child who got to be involved so closely in this movement," she recalled, "I realized I had a great responsibility not just to represent myself but also to represent my generation, and future generations of people with disabilities."

The protestors indeed created a lasting legacy through their actions. Just a few months later, on July 26, 1990, with bipartisan support, President George H. W. Bush made the ADA the law of the land. With Dart by his side, President Bush declared "Let the shameful wall of exclusion finally come tumbling down." In the years since this watershed moment, activists have continued to work toward knocking down that (still rather high) wall.

One year and three days after the signing of the ADA, I came into the world. I fit squarely into the generation of disabled people who grew up with the law's civil rights protections in place. In so many ways, I'm incredibly lucky to have been born when I was, because the movement for disability rights had already come so far. But in the more than three decades that have passed, it's remained evident that we still have so far to go.

In 1995, a Black disabled woman named Lois Curtis became central to the fight for freedom from living in institutions. Joined in 1996 by another disabled woman living in an institution, Elaine Wilson, the two were plaintiffs in a landmark court case that came to be known as the Olmstead decision. The case centered on the right of disabled people to live in the community. By 1999, the case had reached the U.S. Supreme Court, which ruled that the ADA prohibits the unnecessary institutionalization of disabled people. The majority opinion in this landmark case was authored by the late, great Justice Ruth Bader Ginsburg, who asserted that segregating disabled people in institutions "perpetuates unwarranted assumptions that persons so isolated are incapable or unworthy of participating in community life." This was a powerful victory to culminate a century of momentum toward disability rights.

The Twenty-First Century: Progress Continues

The work and legacies of advocates who paved the way for the disability community have continued well into the twenty-first century. The first two decades of the 2000s have been a fast-moving tug-of-war between political and cultural setbacks and hard-won gains. Here's a brief timeline of a few of what I consider to be the most significant events.

- 2002—Vermont becomes the first state to close all sheltered workshops, setting an example by focusing on inclusive employment opportunities for disabled people.
- 2006—The Autistic Self Advocacy Network, an organization run by and for Autistic people, is founded by Autistic leaders Ari Ne'eman and Scott Michael Robertson.
- 2010—President Barack Obama signs the Twenty-First Century Communications and Video Accessibility Act into law, expanding access to a range of digital communication technology for people with disabilities.
- 2011—The United Nations General Assembly recognizes March 21 as World Down Syndrome Day, since held annually.
- 2012—Tammy Duckworth becomes the first visibly physically disabled woman to be elected to the U.S. Senate.
- 2012—The U.S. Senate rejects ratifying the Convention on the Rights of Persons with Disabilities, a United Nations treaty modeled after the Americans with Disabilities Act (ADA), even though it had already been ratified by 126 other countries.
- 2013—Jenny Hatch, a woman with Down syndrome, wins a court victory against her parents, who wanted her to live in a group home instead of leading the life she wanted in her community.
- 2014—The Achieving a Better Life Experience (ABLE) Act passes, which allows disabled people to put money into savings accounts that can be used for authorized purposes without putting their disability benefits at risk.
- 2015—Leah Katz-Hernandez becomes the first deaf receptionist in the West Wing of the White House.

- 2017—The misleadingly named ADA Education and Reform Act is introduced in the House of Representatives, aimed at dismantling enforcement of the ADA. As of this writing, it has passed in the House but not the Senate.
- 2017—Disabled protestors, especially ADAPT members, fight and win the battle to save Medicaid in the face of a Senate bill that proposed deep cuts to funding.
- 2019—Ali Stroker becomes the first wheelchair user to win a Tony Award for her performance in *Oklahoma!* on Broadway.
- 2020—The disability community fights for our existence as politicians, medical professionals, and bioethicists debate the merits of rationing healthcare based on disability status and "preexisting conditions" during the COVID-19 pandemic.

The disability community continues to make progress moment by moment, bit by bit. Activists have devoted blood, sweat, and tears to working toward change, yet there's always more work to be done. And so the wheel(chair)s of history roll on.

Multiple Movements

When we talk about the disability community and its history, we also have to acknowledge who's often left out of these conversations and recognize that those most often excluded are the ones making change and progress happen. Though I refer to the "disability community," remember that we don't exist as one giant cohesive group. While we do have many shared values regarding our rights as human beings, different movements within our community have developed based on the types of discrimination experienced by specific groups of disabled people. These movements do not always operate in unity; in fact, they are sometimes at odds with each other due to the dynamics of who holds power and privilege in our society. When people with different disabilities who identify with different movements work together, this is considered "cross-disability" work.

It is not my intention to erase anyone's experience, and this section is by no means a comprehensive overview of every single disability movement and its history. Rather, it highlights just some of the multiple disability movements that coexist, driving home the larger point that not all people with disabilities are the same, and we are engaged in different fights for our rights.

Independent Living Movement

In 1962, Ed Roberts, who became disabled after contracting polio as a teenager, was the first wheelchair user to be accepted to the University of California, Berkeley. Throughout the decade following his admission to the school, Roberts and a group of his fellow disabled students, known by the catchy name "the Rolling Quads," developed the Physically Disabled Students' Program. This program, which provided services and pushed for accessibility, led to the 1972 establishment of the Berkeley Center for Independent Living—a disability advocacy organization dedicated to providing support for disabled people to thrive in their communities instead of being confined to institutions and nursing homes. And so began a movement. Centers for Independent Living (CILs), which are nonprofit agencies, have since been established to support and empower disabled people to be in control of their own lives, not only across the United States but also around the world.

Reflecting on his work during a *60 Minutes* interview in 1989, Roberts asked, "What's a life living in an institution or a nursing home? Not much of a life. Yet we spend billions and billions of dollars on these. What we have to do is break that money loose from very strong special interests and move it into the community and deal with quality-of-life issues. We do not want to be segregated." And that's exactly what the Independent Living (IL) movement strives for: cross-disability access to life in the community.

The ideology of the IL movement has long been something with which I've closely identified. It is the movement that I came up in as I developed my advocacy. I interned at my local CIL and sat on the board of the National Council on Independent Living. However, I must directly acknowledge that IL has historically been and largely continues to be a predominantly white-led movement that is centered on physically disabled people. Therefore, while I've benefited greatly from and celebrate the work of the movement and those who have shaped it, I recognize that there is much work to be done for it to be truly inclusive of all.

Disability Justice Movement

People who are the most privileged are also the most centered (meaning recognized or prioritized) both in how society understands disability and in many advocacy efforts for disability rights. To shift this reality, the concept of Disability Justice emerged to recognize the intersection of multiple forms of prejudice and discrimination against people of marginalized identities. I frequently see the terms *disability rights* and *disability justice* used interchangeably, but they're not one and the same. Disability Justice is a framework that both builds on and diverges from disability rights, centering marginalized disabled people who are so often left behind in broader conversations about disability rights.

Skin, Tooth, and Bone: The Basis of Movement Is Our People, a powerful primer on Disability Justice from performance project Sins Invalid, more fully breaks down the many people and identities that have for too long been excluded from disability rights–focused work:

> While a concrete and radical move forward toward justice for disabled people, the Disability Rights Movement simultaneously invisibilized the lives of disabled people of color, immigrants with disabilities, disabled people who practice marginalized religions (in particular those experiencing the violence of anti-Islamic beliefs and actions), queers with disabilities, trans and gender non-conforming people with disabilities, people with disabilities who are houseless, people with disabilities who are incarcerated, people with disabilities who have had their ancestral lands stolen, among others.

The Disability Justice movement is a framework through which I can understand my own privilege as a straight white woman, and be in solidarity with disabled people of multiple marginalized identities whose experiences are so often diminished or completely left out of disability rights advocacy. And indeed, recognizing that not all disability experiences are the same is key to Disability Justice. On her blog *Leaving Evidence*, Mia Mingus, writer, educator, and community organizer for Disability Justice, explains that it is about "moving away from an equality-based model of sameness and 'we are just like you' to a model of disability that embraces difference, confronts privilege, and challenges what is considered 'normal' on every front."

Self-Advocacy Movement

The prevailing attitude that much of society has long held regarding people with intellectual and developmental disabilities (I/DD) is that either such individuals are unable to speak for or make decisions for themselves or that they should not do so. This totally incorrect mindset is deeply rooted in the discriminatory belief that cognitive abilities are a determinant of a person's worth, value, and entitlement to civil and human rights. While these misconceptions remain widespread, there is a strong movement dedicated to pushing back against them: the self-advocacy movement.

In 1974, a small group of people with I/DD came together in Oregon and formed the organization People First, so named as a reminder that people with disabilities are *people*, and they should not be defined by their disabilities. It grew into a movement, led by people with disabilities, to fight the patterns of prejudice and harm perpetuated by a society that believed it was better to isolate those with disabilities in institutions rather than support them to live in their communities. In *Lost in a Desert World: An Autobiography*, the late Roland Johnson, a leader in the self-advocacy movement who served as a president of Philadelphia-based group Speaking for Ourselves, urged a shift away from institutions. "People need to be out in a community," he wrote. "Because dollars are spent in an institution—every head is in an institution, a dollar is spent there and not in the community. . . . The services need to be in the community and not in an institution."

Self-advocates have continued to work toward this reality and the movement has expanded steadily, with more than 1,200 local self-advocacy groups across the United States empowering people with disabilities to speak up for themselves and make their own choices. Max Barrows, a self-advocate, has spent well over a decade as part of the self-advocacy movement, working as the outreach director for Green Mountain Self-Advocates and serving multiple terms on the board of Self Advocates Becoming Empowered. "Who knows us better than we know ourselves?" he said to me, more a statement than a question. "People with disabilities need further opportunities to take the lead on work, policies, and decisions about our lives." This means decisions big and small, from choosing what to eat for lunch to choosing friends and romantic partners, from choosing an outfit to deciding where to live. In a world that still largely seems to think it's necessary and acceptable for parents, teachers, guardians, medical professionals, and pretty much everyone *but* people with disabilities to speak on behalf of and make decisions for people with disabilities, the self-advocacy movement is continually changing the game.

Neurodiversity Movement

For far too long, we've been led to believe that people have either "good" brains or "bad" brains, "normal" ones or "abnormal" ones. Neurodiversity is a concept that rejects these morality- and value-based judgments of the human mind, instead embracing the naturally occurring fact that no one's brain is exactly like anyone else's brain. Within the neurodiversity movement, people with disability-related brain differences are referred to as "neurodivergent," while people who don't have such differences are referred to as "neurotypical."

Autistic activist and journalist Sara Luterman shared with me how the neurodiversity movement helped her reframe how she understands herself. "I always had this concept of myself, like maybe I was just a bad person," she said. "People just didn't like me and I didn't understand why, so thinking I was a bad person was the logical progression for me. Neurodiversity gave me the ability to realize that that's not the case. I just have a different kind of brain, but it's morally neutral. There's no good or evil involved."

Though neurodiversity is a framework that everyone can use to understand the natural variations of human brains, it's crucial to recognize that the neurodiversity movement itself is not about neurotypical people. As explained in "Increasing Neurodiversity in Disability and Social Justice Advocacy Groups," a paper by Dr. Jessica M. F. Hughes, "Neurodiversity is a 'big tent' concept that includes every person in the world and centers the experiences of those who are neurodivergent, but the neurodiversity movement is much smaller in scope. Autistic self-advocates are leading the contemporary neurodiversity movement." Neurotypical people need to recognize that the people leading the movement celebrate their neurodivergence—it's not something that needs fixing, or a cure, or to be eliminated. It's simply part of what makes them who they are. In "Don't Mourn for Us," an essay by Autistic activist Jim Sinclair that broke early ground for the neurodiversity movement, Sinclair lamented, "The tragedy is not that we're here, but that your world has no place for us to be."

Psychiatric Survivors Movement

The psychiatric survivors movement, also called the consumer movement and the ex-patient movement, emerged as a response from people with mental illness who, by either choice or coercion,

experienced psychiatric interventions, including institutionalization. When the movement began in the 1970s, it was specifically
led by people identifying as "ex-mental patients," including
Judi Chamberlin, who explains in her book *On Our Own: Patient-
Controlled Alternatives to the Mental Health System*, that they
were "taking a label of shame and attempting to transform it into
one of pride." And pride is a central aspect of the movement for so
many, who push back against stigma and celebrate their identities
by embracing what's known as Mad Pride. Within the broader
movement, people have varying viewpoints on everything from the
name of the movement to whether the mental health care system as it exists today should be reformed (and how) or abolished
altogether. But one core tenet of the movement is clear: Mentally ill
people—not the perspectives of the medical establishment—must
be centered.

Leah Harris, a writer and activist who identifies as a psychiatric survivor, shared with me that one of the most powerful concepts
to come out of the movement is peer support—that is, mutual mental health support provided by people with lived experience. "It's
an innovation and a gift to the world," Harris said. "It's so different
than the existing system of psychiatric care. It's about meeting a
person where they are and providing support that is noncoercive.
It's about holding space and listening nonjudgmentally." And so,
although the broader movement isn't fully united, Harris wants the
world to recognize that "beautiful things have emerged from it."

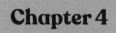

Chapter 4

Ableism
and Accessibility

Staying alive is a lot of work for a disabled person in an ableist society.

— Alice Wong, editor of *Disability Visibility:*
First-Person Stories from the Twenty-First Century

No doubt you're familiar with at least a few of what I call "-isms" and "-phobias"—different types of discrimination against specific groups of people. There's sexism, racism, ageism, homophobia, transphobia, xenophobia . . . unfortunately, we live in a world where the list goes on. But there is often something missing from conversations about discrimination: ableism.

What Is Ableism?

Ableism, as we touched on earlier, is discrimination and prejudice against people with disabilities, though that's not quite enough to convey its full weight. So here's the definition I use. "Ableism is attitudes, actions, and circumstances that devalue people because they are disabled or perceived as having a disability." We'll get to plenty of specific examples of ableism in just a bit; but first, it's helpful to look at the bigger picture. Although the term itself first came into use only in the later part of the twentieth century, ableism has always been a part of our culture. It's so ingrained in society that it can be all too easy to overlook.

Here's the challenge that I always face when trying to explain what ableism actually looks like. Often it's glaringly obvious, but in many cases it's so insidious that it's hard to articulate exactly why something is ableist. And that's the crux of ableism, really. To most of society, ableist beliefs and behavior don't raise any red flags because they're woven into the fabric of everyday life, simply accepted as the norm. For disabled people, though, ableism is always there—a part of our lives that never disappears, manifesting in endless forms ranging from broad, systemic discrimination to individual interactions.

I wish I could say that there are easy solutions to eliminate ableism, but the problem is, it's a self-perpetuating cycle. Here's an example. Less than 25 percent of New York City subway stations have elevators. This is systemic ableism because the lack of accessibility limits the freedom of disabled people to get around. Despite this, I do occasionally brave the subway, but it's not uncommon for me to be the only wheelchair user on the platform. Strangers will express surprise at seeing me there, making ableist comments such as, "Wow, it's amazing how you get around in that chair" or "It's so good to see people like you out." If every subway station had an elevator, it wouldn't be considered anything special to see wheelchair users on the train. But many people operate on the assumption that disabled people don't have full lives that might require public transportation. And if this assumption weren't embedded in society's thinking, making sure every subway station has an elevator would be more of a priority. See what I mean? Ableist assumptions lead to systemic ableism, such as accessibility, which (whether intentional or not) leads to further discrimination.

Think about it. There are still laws on the books that explicitly discriminate against disabled people. As previously stated, the nearly century-old Fair Labor Standards Act was created to be supposedly "fair" for everyone, but people with disabilities are the only population, as named in the law, who can legally be paid far less than the minimum wage. Even worse, this happens in segregated work environments known as "sheltered workshops" where disabled people are paid a few cents per hour to do repetitive tasks—the same tasks that nondisabled people would be paid at least minimum wage to complete in a regular workplace. Though originally intended as an alternative to institutions, it's time for sheltered workshops to be a thing of the past. Need an example of why? In 2019, a New Mexico–based nonprofit organization called Adelante Development Center, which claims to be an organization that "supports . . . disadvantaged populations," was sued for its practice of paying disabled employees a pittance for a day's work. Let's consider this from a social model perspective. People with disabilities aren't inherently disadvantaged; rather, we're put at a disadvantage by practices such as this. One of the things that Adelante's workers had to do was package lipsticks for the 2018 Academy Awards swag bags. If that's not inequality on display, I don't know what is.

Advocates in favor of sheltered workshops and subminimum wages argue that such things are necessary because the disabled people who work in these conditions would otherwise have no job prospects. Organizations that run sheltered workshops (like Goodwill—sorry, thrifters) think they're doing a good deed while getting a good deal on labor. But pennies for piecework isn't acceptable just because the workers are disabled. It's ableist.

Instead of having such low expectations for disabled people, what if we finally left the past behind and demanded fair pay and inclusive workplaces for all?

There are still major companies that don't care if their services are unusable for disabled people. In 2016, a blind man sued Domino's Pizza, arguing that it was in violation of the Americans with Disabilities Act because its mobile app and website were not accessible for use with software that reads the text on a screen. Instead of abiding by court rulings to make its ordering platforms accessible, Domino's tried to push the case all the way up to the U.S. Supreme Court in 2019. Thankfully, the Supreme Court rejected the petition to hear the case, which means the lower court ruling that Domino's must make its app and website accessible stands. But it's pretty frustrating that disabled people have to fight so hard for something as basic as being able to order pizza.

And there are still people in the media industry who think it's not only acceptable but hilarious to use disability as the punchline for their jokes. In 2018, the CEO of Netflix defended a bit on the R-word by nondisabled comedian Tom Segura as "fall[ing] within the bounds of creative expression as part of a stand-up comedy performance." But what might seem like harmless humor isn't funny to disabled people. For that matter, jokes that rely on making fun of people with disabilities shouldn't be considered funny *by anyone*.

Fighting back against ableism in its many iterations feels like playing a never-ending game of whack-a-mole—smack down one instance and it won't be long before another one pops up. It can be exhausting to try to stop such a vicious cycle. While I do believe plenty of nondisabled people are genuinely willing to try to understand ableism, I'm still regularly met with at least some disdain for pointing it out, from people both with and without disabilities. And I'd be remiss if I didn't acknowledge that while I'm shouting about ableism from the rooftops, other people with disabilities may chime in that they disagree. When I come across an article that I interpret as discriminatory toward disabled people, another disabled reader may take no issue with it. On the flip side, I've occasionally been the one to disagree with other disabled people about something or someone being ableist. As difficult as these differences in perception may be, it would be a form of ableism in and of itself to presume that all disabled people share the same opinions. It's simple to use the term *disability community* as a catchall phrase for the population, but that doesn't mean our beliefs exist as a single entity. We're all individuals, and our perspectives vary based on personal experience.

Most of the time, though, it's nondisabled people who take issue with my anti-ableism advocacy. If I speak up about a place that I can't get into because I use a wheelchair, I'm called a complainer. If I mention that a line in a play I've just seen was, in my opinion, ableist, I'm told I'm overthinking things. If I think that a news story about a disabled person overcoming an obstacle is condescending and then comment on it, I'm accused of being bitter and coldhearted.

The "bitter cripple" is a cruel stereotype, a label often metaphorically stamped on the foreheads of disabled people who push back against ableism. Goodness knows I've been given that label a time or two, or several, for saying what's on my mind. But it's not bitterness that drives me; it's my passion to move toward a more accepting, loving, equitable world.

When ableism comes at you from so many directions, it can be challenging to avoid internalizing it. I can't recall a time when I haven't struggled with this in some way. My cheeks have burned red with embarrassment as I asked for help with certain physical tasks. I've apologized when plans needed to change because the place someone suggested has stairs. I've lost sleep over fears that my disability makes me undeserving of being romantically loved. When such thoughts cross my mind, I have to remind myself that my disability does not make me burdensome or embarrassing. If anyone thinks of me that way, that's *their* problem. If I can't go somewhere because of a staircase, that's not my fault. If I need assistance, that's okay. As the Beatles remind us, we *all* get by with a little help from our friends. Disability and all the complexities that come with it do not make a person unworthy.

But ableism takes a heavy toll. Too many disabled people have been led to believe that our very lives are not worth living. And if there's one thing—just *one*—that you take away from reading this book, let it be this: That line of thinking is unequivocally untrue. Disabled lives *are* worth living.

Mind Your Ableism

I need to make a confession. As hard as I fight against ableism, there have most definitely been times when I've been ableist toward other disabled people. And it'll likely happen again. I'm not proud of this, but I believe that being transparent about our missteps is how we make progress. There's no magical force field preventing disabled people from being ableist. We all need to check ourselves to make sure that we're not holding on to ableist ideas and biases. Part of this means recognizing that we can't talk about ableism without acknowledging that it's often deeply inter-connected with other forms of discrimination.

Consider the gutting story of Seven Bridges, a ten-year-old Black boy with a disability who took his own life in 2019 after being subjected to vicious racist and ableist bullying by his classmates. He was attacked with slurs, choked, and mocked for needing an ostomy bag—an external pouch that collects body waste. We can't look at these actions separately; the way this young boy was treated was very much based on the coexistence of his two minority identities. In a blog post for the Disability Visibility Project reflecting on the death of Bridges, Black disabled activist Imani Barbarin calls out the need to "create space for disabled Black, Indigenous, and people of color to feel like they're not alone in all the intersections [they] inhabit." She declares that such work "is lifesaving, and it's time we get to it." It's definitely time for all of us to get to it. Because, sometimes, even people who are devoted to fighting discrimination can end up using tactics that are ableist. An all too common example of this is referring to racist people as mentally ill or calling racism a "sickness" or "disease." The senti-ment that people are trying to express is that racism is BAD, but calling any form of prejudice "a disability" is both dismissive of the issue at hand and an expression of prejudice *against* disability.

We also need to be mindful of the fact that ableism often takes the form of excluding people with disabilities from larger discus-sions of injustice. In 2017, many disability activists, myself included, called on the Women's March to include disability issues as part of their "Unity Principles" because such issues were initially excluded from the March's social justice platform. And as of the writing of this book, the website for TIME'S UP, a movement to fight back against sexual harassment, states "We want every person—across race, ethnicity, religion, sexuality, gender identity, and income level—to be safe on the job and have equal opportunity for economic success and security." No mention of disability, despite the fact that people with disabilities are more than three times as likely as nondisabled people to experience sexual violence. This staggering statistic should be proof enough of why disability must be included in social justice movements. Excluding it isn't just ableist; it's directly contributing to harm.

If you've been ableist, or part of a movement that's excluded disability, I don't want you to feel dismissed for that out of hand. I agree with filmmaker, consultant, and streamer Dominick Evans, who tweeted: "I don't personally like dismissing people for being ableist. It's embedded in our culture, and I had to learn to be better, so how can I expect nondisabled people to know how to be better? What gets me is when people learn the harm they've caused, and double down about it."

This perfectly sums up what I hope you will take away from this book. I believe that you *can* do better. We all can. It's time for everyone to do the hard but important work of unlearning ableism. It's time for awareness of the disability experience to be folded into our conversations about the people and the world around us.

Access and Inaccessibility

When most people think about the word *accessibility* (if they think about it at all), chances are that ramps or elevators are the first things that come to mind. But accessibility encompasses so much more than that. When disabled people can fully use and experience a product or service, that's accessibility. When disabled people can occupy and move about a space freely, that's accessibility. And when accommodations are provided to ensure that both of these things are possible for disabled people, that's accessibility.

Accommodations come in many forms. Examples include:

- Designating quiet rooms with dim lights for people to decompress from sensory overload at events.
- Flexible hours to enable people to work on a schedule that's right for their body.
- Sending a slide deck in advance of a meeting so people have extra time to process the information.
- Providing a combination of live captioning and sign language interpreters to ensure that people with hearing and processing disabilities can follow what's being said during an event.
- Designating seating areas that are easy for people with mobility disabilities to get to and spacious enough for people who use mobility equipment.
- Offering large-print or Braille materials for people with vision disabilities.

Unfortunately, accessibility usually isn't even so much as an afterthought, and it's often overlooked altogether, which is annoying and inconvenient for disabled people, to say the least. Here's how I explain it. Imagine your friends are talking nonstop about a trendy new place in the neighborhood that they want to try. The catch? There's a password to get in.

You all head out for the evening and when you get to the door, your friends simply give the password and are granted access. But when you reach the door, you're told that the password you gave was wrong. Everyone else can enjoy the experience uninhibited. But you? Access denied. Imagine a slightly different scenario. The password worked for the front door; but once you got inside, you found out that there was a second password for the bathroom and no one would give it to you. Can you really be comfortable enjoying an evening out at the trendy new place if you can't use the bathroom there? What if this same scenario kept happening to you at different places because no one could be bothered to share the passwords?

Frustrating, right? But that's often the reality of being disabled. We're shut out or excluded because the world is not designed for us. I experience this constantly and, honestly, it crushes me every time. So I'll let you in on the password that can fix this problem: Accessibility.

Accessibility is about making things more equitable so that disabled people have the same opportunities and support to thrive as do nondisabled people. It's about removing barriers to participation, engagement, and understanding so that all people, regardless of ability, can experience the world around us to the fullest extent possible in ways that work for our minds and bodies. Accessibility is *not* about special treatment or privileges. Sure, I may get to cut to the front of a line every once in a while or pay a discounted entry fee at a museum, but I'd trade these "perks" in a heartbeat if it meant I'd no longer have to enter buildings through a back door next to dumpsters full of garbage because the front entry has only stairs.

Because of inaccessibility, I've been disinvited from hanging out with people who called themselves my friends. I've been on dates that were disastrous because of accessibility issues. I've been turned away everywhere from bars to potential new doctors' offices because of inaccessibility. It's tiring, to say the least. Over and over, I hear the same excuses about why implementing access just isn't possible. *It's too expensive. It's too much effort. It won't look nice. There's not enough time. That's not our job.* And then there's the classic excuse: "People with disabilities don't really visit this location/shop here/apply for jobs with us/attend this event, so what's the point of accessibility anyway?" First of all, I can guarantee that's inaccurate, because many disabilities are non-apparent and people aren't obligated to disclose their disabilities. Second, it's likely that the lack of accessibility is the reason why not many disabled people patronize a particular establishment in the first place.

What people are really saying when they make excuses about accessibility is "Disabled people are unwelcome here." I've been met with these responses so frequently that it's left a wound that never fully heals. It's difficult not to feel as though I'm the burden when I encounter inaccessibility. I constantly have to remind myself that disabled people aren't burdens. Rather, the burden is on us to navigate an inaccessible world. Rebekah Taussig, in her book *Sitting Pretty*, gives voice to the emotional toll of physical inaccessibility:

> Many days, I feel too vulnerable to leave my house, too fed up to subject myself to the gamble of strangers interacting with me, too tired to fight to occupy a corner of space. Inaccessibility over time tells me that I do not matter, I'm not wanted, do not belong. This land wasn't made for me. So I stay in, keep

to myself, avoid, cancel plans, carry anxiety in each fold and bend of my body, feel very alone and trapped and helpless.

It doesn't have to be this way. For that matter, it *shouldn't* ever be this way. Because ensuring accessibility isn't just the right thing to do; it's the law. Unfortunately, far too many people and places have yet to catch up with legal requirements. Inaccessibility remains a widespread systemic issue that's in dire need of fixing.

Having said that, I do understand that making something accessible may feel like an overwhelming responsibility. You might be worried about getting it wrong. And if you're a business owner or employer, you might even be worried about being sued for not complying with the law. But here's the thing; disabled people aren't bad guys out to get you because of inaccessibility. Our goal is to get closer to realizing truly equal access and equal opportunity.

So how do you know where to begin? If you're just starting the journey of figuring out accessibility, there will be a learning curve. After all, accessibility can take many different forms—handrails to hold on to in a bathroom; transcripts for a video or podcast; a website that can be navigated with software that reads text on the screen; using plain, clear language in a document. But I promise it's not actually that complicated to figure out what you need to do.

If you're feeling uncertain about specific access issues, it's often helpful to ask how you can best ensure accessibility rather than making assumptions. Of course, I don't mean to give anyone carte blanche to pepper disabled people with invasive questions. A good first step is to do some research on your own. Two of my go-to resources for finding answers are the ADA National Network and the Job Accommodation Network (JAN), both of which provide free information and guidance on a variety of topics and can help clear up lots of your accessibility questions. If you do happen to be connected with disabled people who are willing to share some insight about particular accommodations that would work for them and people with similar disabilities, they can be a good information source. That said, be considerate of the fact that picking someone's brain is requiring work from *them*. If you have substantive questions and a budget, I highly recommend hiring a (disabled) accessibility consultant with expertise in the specific accessibility area on which you're focused.

In many cases, though, you'll find that there are free or relatively low-cost workable solutions for access. It can be as simple as buying a portable ramp to go over a few steps, or asking event attendees to not use heavily scented body products so that people with scent sensitivities can breathe freely. What's *not* a solution is saying things such as, "Can't someone just read all the handouts to you?" or "Oh, we can just carry you up the stairs." (A "solution" I've been given many times as a wheelchair user.) "Solutions" such as these don't fix the problem—they are *part* of the problem.

The real solution is recognizing that everyone can play a role in eliminating inaccessibility, and that eliminating inaccessibility benefits everyone. A concept known as the "curb-cut effect" highlights this quite well. While curb cuts were initially designed for wheelchair users, anyone can use them—and many people find them helpful. Think about it: baby strollers, shopping carts, wheeled suitcases, roller skates. Curb cuts really come through in lots of situations. What the world needs to eliminate both inaccessibility and ableism is more curb cuts—both literally and figuratively.

Indeed, accessibility is a key step toward inclusivity. That trendy little spot in the neighborhood that I mentioned earlier? For me, it was a local coffee shop with an inaccessible entrance (though it's happened at so many different places). I decided to call the phone number posted on the door, hoping that I'd reach the owners and convince them to put a ramp in place. When I first got in touch, they seemed caught up in the chaos of opening a new business but promised a ramp was to come. I was hopeful, but definitely skeptical. Several months later, I got a phone call. The owner had finally gotten a portable ramp, and they'd held on to my phone number to let me know. I had such a mix of emotions after that call, wondering why it had taken so long, but feeling grateful that they'd even thought to reach out and personally invite me in. It was a gesture unlike anything a business owner had ever done for me before. While I believe accessibility should be prioritized from the start, I also believe in appreciating accessibility wins. And to me, this was definitely a win.

What Does Ableism Look Like?

The stories of ableism I've experienced in my lifetime could easily have filled every page of this book and then some. But ableism isn't just my story. It's a common thread that runs through the disabled experience that could fill volumes. There's simply no way to cover it all. My hope is that sharing this brief list of examples will awaken you to just how deep-seated ableism is in every part of our society, and that you'll begin to recognize both blatant and subtle ableist patterns.

- In two-thirds of the United States there are statutes in place that allow courts to deem a parent unfit on the basis of their disability, which means their parental rights can be terminated.
- Rideshare drivers regularly refuse rides to people who use mobility equipment or have a service animal.
- During the 2015–2016 school year in the United States, a mere 16.6 percent of students with intellectual disabilities were included in general education classes about 80 percent of the time. The rest of the time they were segregated.
- Because Autistic kids are largely expected to adhere to arbitrary ideas of what's "normal," they are often subjected to potentially harmful behavioral therapy to either reinforce or quell certain behaviors.
- Hundreds of thousands of people with disabilities, especially with intellectual and developmental disabilities, are still forced to live in institutionalized settings instead of in their communities.

- Disabled people are frequently excluded from participating in large group meetings and events because of a lack of accessibility supports such as interpreters, live captioning, and Braille, large-print, or digitized materials.
- The median income for Americans with disabilities is less than 70 percent of the median earnings of those without a disability.
- Nondisabled people, especially medical professionals, often assume people with disabilities want to be "fixed" or "cured" instead of living with their disability.
- Since 2015, more than eight hundred disabled people, worldwide, have been murdered by their caregivers. Media outlets often report on these cases using language that shows sympathy for the killers, framing it as though caregivers were relieving themselves of a burden.
- During the COVID-19 pandemic, many states and countries issued guidelines explicitly calling for disabilities to be taken into account as a reason to *not* provide lifesaving health care to sick people.
- A 2013 survey conducted by the United Nations Office for Disaster Risk Reduction found that out of 5,717 respondents with disabilities, from 137 countries, a staggering 85.57 percent were excluded from the disaster management and risk reduction processes in place in their communities.

I know that even this small collection of examples may seem overwhelming, but remember, the first step in fighting back against ableism is awareness.

Chapter 5

Disability Etiquette 101

Overthinking is one enemy of disability etiquette, but so is making assumptions about what a person wants and needs. Of course disabled people want to be treated like everyone else, but when we say that, we don't mean "treat every person exactly the same." We mean "recognize our humanity and meet us where we're at."

— Kyle Khachadurian, cohost, *The Accessible Stall* podcast

We've talked a lot about big, systemic instances of ableism, but what about everyday interactions? How can we avoid perpetuating ableism? The key is acquainting yourself with *disability etiquette*, which is the go-to term for the title of just about every guide I've ever read on how to interact with people with disabilities. I worry that "etiquette" comes across a bit too formal, though. After all, my name is Emily Ladau, not Emily Post (the famed etiquette expert). I don't want people to think that engaging with me or any disabled person requires learning a comprehensive set of rules and regulations. Really, proper disability etiquette comes down to one simple piece of timeless wisdom: the Golden Rule. Treat others as you want to be treated. I think it's safe to say you wouldn't want someone to be condescending, nosy, rude, or downright mean to you, right? Keep this in mind as we go over the do's and don'ts of disability decorum. And please remember that while I offer stories and examples, this section can't account for every possible circumstance. Take these as tips to apply to all your interactions with disabled people.

You don't need to start overthinking everything you say or do. That just makes things weird. Disability etiquette isn't about tiptoeing around us and treating us like strange, delicate flowers. (In fact, that's pretty ableist in and of itself.) It's about treating us like full and equal human beings.

Disability Etiquette Do's

As you dive into these etiquette do's, keep in mind the common thread that runs through them: Respect. Careless words and actions can hurt, but being thoughtful about what you say and what you do can make a world of positive difference.

Do Keep Your Nosy Questions, Rude Comments, and Unsolicited Advice to Yourself

I'm not exaggerating when I tell you that I can't leave my house without at least one person saying something to me about my wheelchair. I'll be rolling along, minding my own business, and inevitably, someone passing by will say some variation of the following:

- Don't run me over!
- Slow down, speed racer!
- You got a license for that thing?
- You're gonna get a speeding ticket!

And every time, the individual says it with a look on their face like they're the first person who's ever made the joke. I hate to burst anyone's comedy bubble but I can guarantee that disabled people have heard it all before. The award for taking a joke like this too far goes to a man who saw my mom and me rolling side by side down a hallway and proceeded to block our path to the exit while making flag motions and demanding we race for him. Despite our telling him to leave us alone multiple times, he followed us to our car and insisted he was sorry to have offended us. As the cherry on top, when we were about to drive away, he tried to offer twenty dollars to my dad as an apology and then flipped us off when we refused to accept it. Do I need to explain why you shouldn't be like this guy?

Rude questions that totally invade the privacy of disabled people are just as common as these kinds of "jokes." I can't begin to count how many times I've been asked (frequently inappropriate) questions by people who definitely don't need to know the answers. In high school, a guy I had a crush on asked me how I put on my pants. Dudes on dating apps have asked if I am physically able to have sex before so much as saying hello. Strangers blurt out, "Can you walk?" while we're in the elevator together. It's exhausting to feel as though I have to answer to the world. And worse, sometimes these kinds of questions are more than nosy. They're harmful. Andrew Gurza, a disability awareness consultant, vividly recalls when one of his high school gym teachers approached him while he was in the middle of doing physical therapy and nonchalantly said, "Hey there, Andrew, what is your life expectancy?" Talk about rude and insensitive. "I was fifteen at the time, and I was so extremely embarrassed," Gurza shares. "I had never had to consider my own mortality before. I was so angry, I left her classroom crying. All the other kids saw me leave. I was mortified."

Curiosity may be part of human nature, but please remember that you're not entitled to information just because someone is disabled, especially if you don't have any level of familiarity with that person. People with disabilities don't exist to be, as Autistic activist

Jim Sinclair phrased it, "self-narrating zoo exhibits." So if you're not sure whether you should ask something, here's a good rule to follow: If you wouldn't ask a nondisabled person the same question in the same context, don't ask a disabled person.

Along with avoiding unnecessary comments and questions, please check yourself before offering unsolicited advice. It's a familiar inside joke among many physically disabled people that when we talk about things such as chronic pain, muscle weakness, or joint stiffness, someone is always waiting in the shadows to jump out and share what they think are helpful solutions. "Have you tried yoga?" "You should do acupuncture!" "My sister's dry cleaner knows a guy who runs a retreat that can totally fix you." I know that people who say such things are well-meaning, but it can feel really patronizing. Just as you're the expert on your own body, disabled people are the experts on ours.

My advice? Whether you identify as disabled or not, if you have a legitimate suggestion and want to share it with another disabled person, prefacing it with something like "Can I share with you what worked for me?" makes a big difference in how it comes across. And if the person says no thanks, leave it at that.

Do Ask Questions When Appropriate

I know we just went over what kind of questions to absolutely avoid, but there's an important distinction between rude questions and acceptable ones. The difference depends on both the context in which the question is being asked and your relationship with the person you're asking. Let's consider a few different scenarios.

Sometimes questions arise because people are genuinely seeking information. For example, I'm occasionally approached in public by strangers who are curious to know specific details about my power wheelchair or my wheelchair-accessible vehicle, usually because they or someone they know would benefit from the information. I'm happy to answer questions like these because I know that information about adaptive equipment isn't always easy to come by. But not everyone is as comfortable engaging, which is okay. So if you have a legitimate question that doesn't unnecessarily invade a disabled person's privacy, it's best to approach and say, "May I ask you a question about . . ." instead of just blurting it out. If the person expresses that they'd prefer not to answer, it might feel awkward, but you can simply say, "Okay, I understand," and move on.

There are also plenty of instances in which the best etiquette is to ask, rather than to avoid, disability-related questions. When you're planning an event, meeting, or outing, it should be standard practice to ask about accessibility needs, even if you're not sure whether other people involved identify as disabled. If you have a certain level of familiarity with the people you're communicating with, the ask can be informal ("Hey, do you/does anyone have any accessibility needs to participate? Let me know how I can support you!"). If you're engaging with someone you don't really know or have a more formal relationship, it can help to add a little more context to what you're asking ("I want to make sure what I'm planning works for you. Is there anything I can do or any accommodations you might need to make this accessible so you can fully participate?").

Things get more personal when it comes to closer relationships. Friends and partners may have questions about certain aspects of disability, in either getting-to-know-you conversations or deeper, more intimate discussions. In these contexts, asking thoughtful questions about someone's disability can be a way to show that you care about the person and want to better understand who they are. Or it might educate you on how to offer support or assistance. If you're unsure how to broach the question, it can help to preface it with something like, "Is it okay if I ask a question about your disability?" or "I'm wondering about [insert whatever you're wondering about]. Would you be up for talking about it?" Take that initial moment to check in with the person to make sure they're comfortable. Open communication about personal aspects of identity is an ongoing process of building trust, so if someone lets you know they'd rather not respond to a disability-related question, please respect that and don't push them on it.

Do Keep Your Hands to Yourself

Respecting personal space is a good rule for human interaction in general, but the rule all too often seems to go out the window when it comes to interacting with people with disabilities.

In my case, strangers and people I don't know well will lean on my wheelchair like it's their personal armrest. It might seem harmless but my wheelchair is an extension of my body and how I move; so when someone puts their weight on it, I feel trapped—even if I'm not actually sitting it in. When I was a student, I used to get out of my wheelchair and keep it next to my desk, and I had a teacher who would lean on it during his lectures. It made me so uncomfortable, but I felt like I couldn't say anything.

Try imagining this without the wheelchair. Would you just go up to any ol' person and lean on them like they're a human wall? Of course, if you know the person well, the etiquette can be different here. I personally don't mind if my friends lean on my chair. But everyone who uses mobility equipment has different preferences, so if you're not sure if it's okay to lean or hold on to someone's, just ask. And if you're told that it's not, then please don't.

The same logic applies to moving a person's mobility equipment without asking first. If you see someone pushing themselves in a manual wheelchair, even if it appears as though they could use some help, don't just come up from behind and start pushing. It's really startling to have someone try to take control of your source of movement. Again, try imagining this scenario without the wheelchair. Would you just go up to someone, put your hands on them, and start to push them? I doubt it. So please make sure you always ask first, and always heed the response you're given.

Touch may also be uncomfortable for disabled people who have sensory sensitivities, which can make social situations a challenge to navigate. Handshakes, hugs, and casual touches while conversing are often instinctual, but instead of just sticking out your hand or throwing your arms around a person, ask first. I tend to be a hugger, but I know that's not the case for everyone. When I'm greeting someone or saying good-bye, I try to pause and ask, "Are you a hugger or more of a handshake person? Neither is okay too!" Some people go for fist bumps, elbow bumps, or high fives. And others just say no thanks to all of it. Give people an option to be comfortable instead of forcing them to go along with social norms.

Unwelcome touch is also a big issue for service animal teams—the animal and their handler. People tend to be particularly eager to say hi when they see service dogs, petting them in spite of the fact that the dog usually wears a vest that explicitly says something along the lines of "Working. Do Not Pet." As a total dog person, I absolutely understand the desire to pet every very good dog you meet. But service dogs are concentrating on a job for which they've trained hard: supporting their handler. Petting them breaks their concentration, and that's *not* okay. It can even be dangerous. If a service dog is guiding their blind handler down a busy sidewalk and you pet them, the dog might lose awareness of obstacles in the surrounding area that could pose a risk to their handler. Or if a service dog is working to detect a drop or spike in their handler's blood sugar, or is on alert for an approaching seizure, petting the dog could be a distraction from giving a timely warning signal. Professor and Paralympian Dr. Anjali Forber-Pratt, a manual wheelchair user, is unfortunately all too used to people trying to pet her service dog, Kolton. "When he is working and somebody goes to pet him, it is a problem because it confuses him. He then thinks that it is off-duty play time and will be paying more attention to the person trying to pet him than to me. If he is in the middle of a task for me, like carrying something, he might drop it, and we have to start the command sequence over again. Don't pet service dogs when they are working!" If you truly can't resist the urge to pet the dog, Dr. Forber-Pratt advises, "Always ask the handler first. Sometimes there are occasions when Kolton is off duty and it is allowed during play time, but it's important to respect the handler's wishes!"

Do Communicate with Disabled People As You Would with Anyone Else

Talking to disabled people, especially those who are visibly disabled or intellectually disabled, seems to put a lot of people on edge. Sometimes I can practically see the discomfort coming off a person, like smoke from a fire, as they worry about not just what to say but how to say it. The simplest advice I have for these concerns? Communicate with a disabled person as you would with anyone else. To start, in every circumstance, please talk *directly to* people with disabilities. If you have something to say to a visibly disabled person who's accompanied by someone else, there's no need to say it to the other person or talk as though the disabled person isn't there.

Writer and activist Kings Floyd, who uses a wheelchair, didn't miss a beat when I asked if she'd ever experienced someone speaking to the person she was with instead of to her. She and her sister, Isabel, who is nondisabled, went out for what was supposed to be a fun night of dinner and an improv show, only to have their server ruin it with her assumption that Floyd couldn't communicate for herself. "She took Isabel's order first and then asked her 'What is she having?,' referring to me," Floyd recounted. "Isabel remained silent, looking intently at the waitress and then at me. I coolly answered 'I'd like the carbonara, please, with mushrooms. I'll also have a lemonade and a side Caesar salad. We are still thinking about dessert.' The waitress nodded, uninterested and avoiding eye contact." Floyd went on, "Later, when she came back with the check, she handed it to Isabel after I had already clarified I was paying. Thankfully, the improv show was amazing and saved the night, but the waitress's tactless assumptions left me feeling truly disrespected, as though she believed my voice didn't matter." But Floyd's voice absolutely did matter, and the server should have treated her with the same respect that she would have given any other customer.

Respect and directness are always key. Conchita Hernández Legorreta, a blind activist, shared with me how important it is to introduce yourself directly when striking up a conversation with someone who's blind, rather than jumping into talking and assuming they might know you by voice. "Say your name before speaking," she says. "[Making] a blind person guess who you are is super-rude. Also keep in mind that many people with low vision can see some things but faces are still very difficult, so do not assume we know who you are." It's as simple as saying, "Hi, it's [full name] speaking."

It's also important to be mindful of personal space when approaching a person who is blind or deaf. You don't want to rush up to someone or startle them. If you're not able to get the person's attention vocally, the conventional advice is to tap them lightly on the shoulder. But there are other ways to make yourself known without touching, which many people prefer. Christine Liao, a deaf advocate, shared that she'd rather the "two most common ways folks suggest to get a deaf person's attention—a tap on the shoulder or flickering the lights—be saved as a last resort." Instead, Liao recommends "getting in the d/Deaf person's line of vision and making a gesture, like a wave, to let them know you are there and wanting to communicate."

When communicating with a deaf person who has a sign language interpreter, look at the person you're talking to rather than the interpreter. You're not having a conversation with the interpreter, and their job isn't to relay information for you; it's to provide translation in order to facilitate a conversation. There's no need to say to an interpreter, "Can you please tell them . . . ?" Just start having your conversation and the interpreter will convey what you're saying. If there's no interpreter available, grab a pen and paper or type on your phone so you can have a direct conversation.

And what about starting a conversation with a person who is d/Deafblind? Elsa Sjunneson, a partially Deafblind author and activist, told me that people often assume she can't engage in lively conversation, which simply isn't true. "The best ways to get my attention," she says, "are to speak clearly (not shouting) and say 'excuse me' or 'hello.' It can also help if you wave your hand in my visual field, but it depends on where I'm sitting." If neither of these are ideal options, Sjunneson advises asking for someone who knows both you and the deafblind person to make an introduction.

If you're talking with a person who stutters or speaks slowly, or who uses a communication aid such as a letter board to spell out words or an electronic device that they type on, please don't attempt to rush them or play guessing games as to what they're trying to say. Eva Sweeney, a sex educator who has cerebral palsy and uses a laser pointer attached to a baseball cap to spell out words on a letter board, offers a straightforward reminder. "Just talk to us like you would anyone else," she explains. "You might have to wait to hear our response, but it is not that different than talking to someone who is verbal! People communicate in a variety of ways, so be open-minded to new ways of communicating and connecting with someone."

If you're having a conversation with someone who is much shorter in stature than you are, or who is lower in height because they're sitting in a wheelchair, consider where you are in relation to their personal space. Are you hovering so close that the person has to crane their neck upward just to look at you? If so, try to take a step or two back to even things out. If you can find a place to sit so that you're closer to the other person's eye level, go for it. Many shorter disabled people, myself included, also generally don't mind if someone bends down or kneels to be closer to eye level, but it's best to ask if that's preferred to avoid coming across as patronizing. And there's certainly no need to make a big show out of it. Once, at a fancy event, a woman in stilettos insisted on crouching down to make small talk with me, which resulted in a few very awkward minutes of watching her fight to keep her balance.

If you're speaking with someone who has a cognitive disability or an information-processing disability, use clear, concise words and sentences, and offer explanations of longer words or jargon if need be. Unless someone specifically asks you to speak at a higher volume or a slower pace to ensure that they can understand what you're saying, there's no need to talk unusually loudly and/or slowly. There's also no need to change the pitch or tone of your voice. It'll only make you look silly at best or condescending at worst, and it won't actually help a disabled person understand you any better.

If you remember only one communication etiquette tip, let it be this: There isn't one "right way" to communicate with anyone, regardless of disability. We're so often taught that there are rules for communicating effectively—firm handshakes, direct eye contact, responsive facial expressions and body language, and so on.

However, these so-called skills aren't always accessible to disabled people, and we shouldn't expect them as the norm. Really, the best way to communicate with any disabled person is simply to not overthink or try too hard. Be open and receptive to different communication styles, and, most important, just be yourself.

Disability Etiquette Don'ts

Just as with the etiquette do's, respect is the central theme of etiquette don'ts.

Don't Talk Down to Disabled People

A common thread running through poor disability etiquette is infantilization: treating people as though they're significantly below their actual age. Disabled kids being spoken to as if they're babies, disabled adults being called "cute" or getting patted on the head. Such treatment is rampant toward people with developmental disabilities, including intellectual disabilities, Autism, and other disabilities that affect communication or thinking, notes Julia Bascom, executive director of the Autistic Self Advocacy Network. She shines a light on the fact that people in these communities are often seen as incapable of thinking, learning, or making their own choices. "But that just isn't true," she says. "That belief is dehumanizing, and responsible for a huge amount of mistreatment." To combat this stigma, the developmental disabilities community embraces a crucial core value: presume competence. "The reality is that people with developmental disabilities, including people with the most significant disabilities, have rich and complex inner lives," Bascom explains. "No matter how significant our disability is, we can and do learn, think, and feel. We might do these things differently, or more slowly, or with more effort compared to other people. Our complexity and competence may not be obvious in ways that people expect. We might need a lot of support. Presuming competence is the idea that, regardless of these things, we are fully human with the same rights as everyone else and, with the right support, we can express ourselves, participate in our communities, and make our own decisions."

Building on this, it's pretty common for people to make generalized assumptions about disability, painting all disabled people with the same broad brush of stigma. So they might look at a person who has a visible physical disability, mistakenly assume that the person is also cognitively disabled, and treat that person in a condescending way. The problem with this isn't misreading what type of disability someone has, but rather using stereotypes about cognitive disabilities as justification for being patronizing. You shouldn't be condescending to *anyone* based on prejudiced assumptions. Everyone deserves to be treated with dignity and respect, simply because they are human.

It comes down to this: Don't make assumptions about what people can and can't do. And remember that we all do and process things differently.

Don't Try to Help without Asking First

Putting on a jacket is a bit of a process for me. I hold it in front of my body, wiggle my right arm into the right sleeve, flip the whole thing over my head, slide my left arm part of the way into the left sleeve, reach for the bottom left side with my right arm, and pull until my arm is all the way through. It's not necessarily the easiest method, and it must look pretty dysfunctional to outside observers. But I've put on a jacket enough times in my life that I've got it figured out and under control. And yet, it's as if the process creates a magnetic field that draws in eager helpers—often strangers—who grab my jacket without asking. Plenty of people just shrug when I try to explain how often this happens, telling me that it's a nonissue and I should accept the help because the people trying to assist mean well. It's just an act of kindness, they say, and I should stop complaining.

As someone who tries to see the good in everyone, I genuinely want to celebrate people helping one another. And I do believe that for most people, trying to help is instinctual. But it's unsettling to have people enter my personal space and interrupt a process that's second nature to me. Plus, they usually end up making it more difficult, but I feel like I have to grin and bear it because pushing the person away would make me seem rude. You know what's actually pretty rude, though? Foisting help on a person without first asking whether they need it, or what they do need.

That said, I will acknowledge that my physical appearance likely plays a role in how often people try to help me. As a petite young white woman, chances are that people perceive me not only as a "damsel in distress" but also as approachable and nonthreatening. I recognize this isn't everyone's experience. Once, while waiting for a train in New York City, I noticed an elderly Black man in ripped clothing and a dilapidated wheelchair ask at least fifteen passersby to help him hang his tote bag on the back of his chair. As he called out for assistance, he was jangling a cup of coins.

Instead of taking just a moment out of their day to help, as people so often do for me even when I'm not asking, every person kept walking as though they hadn't heard him. I found it interesting that the man didn't ask me for help, even though I was nearby, perhaps because I'm a wheelchair user as well and he wasn't sure if I could assist. When I realized no one else was stopping, I approached to ask if I might be able to do what he needed, and he accepted. And while I was happy to help, it shouldn't have come to that. Snap judgments rooted in stigma shouldn't be a justifiable reason for so many people to ignore such a simple request.

On the flip side, however, are those whose snap judgments about people with apparent disabilities mean they won't take no for an answer if they offer help. Walei Sabry, a blind disability rights activist, knows this all too well. He and a classmate who is also blind were walking to the train together one day after class when, as he says, "All of a sudden, out of nowhere, two strangers decided to take it upon themselves to help us. Without saying any-thing, they each grabbed one of us. I started to ask the man who grabbed me to let go, telling him that we were fine. They insisted on helping and there was a back and forth for a few minutes. The gentleman that grabbed me finally said, 'I don't understand. We are just trying to help you.' To which I replied, 'We didn't ask for your help!' They finally got the point but they weren't happy about it. As the man walked away, he yelled, 'You two are the worst blind people in New York!'" Remember the etiquette "do" about keeping your hands to yourself? That definitely should have applied here!

Don't escalate your offers of help to this point. Remember, disabled people are the experts on what they need. This is crucial to consider when someone you know is experiencing a mental health crisis. As Leah Harris, who identifies as a psychiatric survivor, shared with me, helping a person in crisis doesn't mean stepping in and trying to fix things in a way that you assume is correct. Instead, they advise, "Ask the person what they need in that moment, or how you can support them. And if the person is not able to articulate that, then you can offer some suggestions. If you have lived experience, you can offer to share with the person what helps you in similar moments. But please, avoid the urge to 'fix' and make it better without first centering what the person in crisis wants and needs."

Don't Stare, but Don't Make a Point of Looking Away

I often joke that it's hard to miss me in a crowd because I have a tank (a four-hundred-plus-pound power wheelchair) attached to my butt. Living life on wheels means that I don't know what it feels like to not be noticeable. I've learned to be comfortable with visibility, but it has been made clear to me over and over that plenty of people aren't comfortable with me. In my case, I do think some of the prolonged stares to which I'm subjected are a result of fascination with my wheelchair, since it's powerful and purple. Honestly, I think it's pretty cool. But more often than not, I'm on the receiving end of double takes and prolonged, uncertain looks. And if I'm out and about with another visibly disabled person (like my mom), the way people tend to stare makes us feel as if we might as well have just escaped from the circus. It's tiring to feel like I'm always on display.

Disabled people are constantly subjected to gawking for simply existing in the world. For example, people are often stared at for "stimming," making repetitive movements or sounds. The book *Welcome to the Autistic Community* explains: "People stim for all sorts of reasons. We stim to help balance out our senses, show how we feel, or focus on things. Stimming can help us feel better, and it's also a great way to have fun." So stimming isn't a weird or bad thing; staring is. Pamela Rae Schuller, a stand-up comedian who has Tourette syndrome, a neurological disorder characterized by repetitive involuntary movements and vocalizations called tics, knows how it feels to be gawked at. "People stare, laugh, point, ask questions, and even try to record me," she says. "Through my comedy, I'm trying to help people become more comfortable with differences. But every now and again I lose my cool. Once, when a woman started videotaping me on the subway, I took out my phone and taped her back. If I ended up on the internet, I wanted to definitively know the face of who put me there, somebody who was all too comfortable causing me pain and making fun of me because of my disability."

Similarly painful is when a person takes a glimpse and looks away as though they can't stand the sight of disability. In her book *Say Hello*, Carly Findlay, an appearance activist who has a skin condition called ichthyosis, shares, "I can't think of a day outside of the house when I haven't been stared at, intruded upon, or abused because of my appearance. Sometimes people look away—which can hurt as much as the stares."

If a person's visible difference or behavior catches your eye, that's okay, but really, there's no need to make a big show of either staring or turning away. While it's simply best to act as you would passing by any other person on the street, if you do happen to be caught staring, smile, move on, and do better next time.

Don't Pray over Disabled People

Encountering stigma disguised as religious belief is practically
a rite of passage for a disabled person. A few years after grad-
uating college, I traveled to interview for a dream job, staying
overnight in a hotel. In the morning, after amping myself up in
the mirror, I went down to the hotel lobby to eat breakfast and go
over my talking points. As I reached for a bowl of cereal, a young
girl and her mom offered to help (+1 etiquette point). I accepted
the help, thanked them, and pulled out my notes. Instead of walking away, the girl lingered and said, "Mommy, can I pray for her?"
(–1 etiquette point for not asking me directly, –1,000 etiquette
points for the following action). She proceeded to pray for Jesus to
heal me, while everyone else in the lobby watched uncomfortably
and I made a concerted effort not to choke on my orange juice.
When she finished, I muttered a thank-you and made a quick exit.
I was mortified.

As I headed to my interview, I tried to laugh off the absurdity
of the whole encounter. I mean, even if nothing else about it was
funny, I was amused because I'm Jewish! But I felt like a deflated
balloon. There I was, preparing for a big moment, mustering all
the confidence I had, only to be snapped out of it with a reminder
that people believe my body is a mistake, my existence is wrong. I
pulled it together and nailed the interview; but all these years later,
I still wish I could find that girl and her mother to take back the
thank-you I gave them, to let them know that in spite of the religious model lens through which they viewed my disability, I'm not
broken and I don't need prayers to be fixed.

Don't Assume Someone's Disability Status

We're socialized to understand nondisabled as the default state of humanity, which means that unless someone "looks" disabled, we generally assume they aren't. I'm totally guilty of this, and it's a mindset that I'm actively trying to shift. I challenge you to take all your stereotypical preconceived notions about what disability does or doesn't look like and throw them out the window. Skip the assumptions and instead focus on incorporating disability etiquette, and prioritizing accessibility, into all your interactions. And remember, whether someone is disabled or not is private information that they are under no obligation to reveal, so ask appropriate questions only when necessary.

Unfortunately, many people make assumptions about whether someone is actually disabled or if they're "faking." One particularly common way this arises is in relation to accessible parking spaces. Paralympian Lacey Henderson, an amputee, has definitely been mistaken as nondisabled before. She recalls, "When I was in college, I drove a green Volkswagen Beetle, wore big sunglasses, and blasted music wherever I went. Once, I was running to return a library book and a woman accosted me at my car, shouting that I was in an accessible spot. I had put my placard up already, but maybe she didn't see it. I was like, 'I have a prosthetic leg,' and she acted as though I really inconvenienced her, because how in the world could a cute girl in a little car who is enjoying life also have a disability that qualifies her to have a placard? Of course, as a young woman in my twenties, I was apologetic (because we're taught to be accommodating and not let people feel uncomfortable with us), but I wish I had been told by someone that I didn't owe any of these people any answers."

Henderson is correct. Disabled people don't owe answers to *anyone*. But we all owe everyone the courtesy of not making assumptions about their disability status. That said, if someone does have a disability that's evident, going out of your way to pretend that you're assuming they're not disabled isn't cool either. I'm not saying that you have to go out of your way, unprompted, to explicitly acknowledge that you recognize someone is disabled, but, if it comes up in conversation, there's no need to duck the mention of it like you would an incoming water balloon.

Don't Use Accessible Amenities if You Don't Need Them

Imagine needing to be somewhere, pulling into a parking lot, and not being able to find a spot. Or really having to use the bathroom but a stall isn't available. Or going to a show and finding that you have nowhere to sit. For nondisabled people, these might be occasional minor frustrations, but for many disabled people, such situations are a constant reality. Necessities such as accessible parking spots, bathroom stalls, and seating are in high demand and limited supply. To mitigate this, disabled people often expend extra effort planning ahead for outings and ensuring they arrive early to where they're going. While most nondisabled people can just pick up and go as they please, I have to calculate backward from the time I'm supposed to be somewhere to figure out how much time I'll need to factor in for potential accessibility issues such as parking, using the restroom, locating an elevator, or finding seating. So using an accessible amenity when you don't actually need it means you're potentially blocking access for some-one who truly does need it. That said, remember to not assume a person's disability status if they are occupying accessible spaces. It's not only people with visible disabilities who need them.

In the case of bathrooms, I can understand using the accessible stall if you have a baby stroller, or even if all the other stalls are occupied and you just really have to go. But it's not there just because you want more room for your luggage, you need to change your outfit and put on your makeup, or you want to cram four people in there at once. If you don't *need* the accessible stall and you occupy it anyway, especially if there are other available stalls, you're creating an unnecessary barrier for people who must use the accessible stall. And if there's a long line for the bathroom and the accessible stall is the only one available but you don't urgently need it, it's generally best to ask down the line if anyone needs that specific stall before you go to use it.

What's never okay is parking in an accessible spot if you don't have a permit to do so. I've heard every excuse—"I was only running in for a minute" or "I'm just waiting for someone and I was going to move." Nope. Not cool. Equally bad is when people make their own spaces by parking in the blue lines between accessible parking spots. The blue lines aren't a make-your-own-parking-spot option. They're there to leave room for people to get in and out of vehicles with permits. And when people flout the rules, there's a good chance a disabled person will be stranded because they're blocked from getting into their vehicle. Don't do this.

Don't Pretend You "Get It"

As a generally empathetic person, I really value people who take the time to listen and try to understand another person's experiences and emotions. But when it comes to disability, I've had far too many encounters with people who instead act as if they understand what I'm "going through" or that they "get it," only for it to come across as a patronizing, pitying kind of sympathy.

I spoke with Maddy Ruvolo, a transportation planner who is chronically ill, about the ways in which people respond when she talks about her disability. "There have been many occasions when I tell people I have chronic fatigue," she says, "and they are like, 'Ugh, yeah, I get so tired, maybe I have that too.' I know it comes from a place of trying to relate, but it feels very dismissive of my experience." Being flippant and cavalier is definitely not the best route to take, but neither is pouring on the sympathy. "Sometimes, people respond by saying things like, 'Oh I'm so sorry,'" Ruvolo said. "I know they're coming from a good place, but I'd rather not be in a position of having to say 'Oh, yeah it's totally fine' and assuage their feelings." People sharing their experiences shouldn't have to make you feel better about their experiences. Ruvolo notes that a better way to respond can be as simple as, "Thank you for sharing."

And remember, you can be empathetic without pretending you know what an experience is like. *"I broke my leg once and needed to use a wheelchair for a month, and wow it was so hard to do things and get around. I totally know what you're dealing with."* I've had several variations of this sentiment expressed to me, and it always leaves me feeling cold. People who say things like this don't seem to recognize that there's a very big difference between an injury they can recover from and a disability. You might experience issues with inaccessibility while recovering from a broken leg, sure, but that doesn't add up to a lifetime of access barriers and discrimination. I really believe people mean well, but here are my questions for them: What are you doing with your newfound insight to the disability experience? Will you advocate for accessibility? Will you fight stigma? To be honest, your temporary experience doesn't mean you "get it," but it does mean you can be a more aware supporter to the disability community.

What about Curious Kids?

Disability etiquette is a whole different ball game for young children, whose boundless curiosity can make for some pretty interesting moments, to say the least. Kids frequently stare at people who look different than the people in their lives, or blurt out questions or comments that would be cringeworthy if they knew better. Personally, I've never minded questions from kids because that's how they learn about the world around them. And sometimes it can be pretty amusing.

I've been on the receiving end of curiosity from kids countless times, and usually I embrace it. I'm comfortable with these teachable moments and am glad to engage as long as it seems okay to do so. But not all disabled people feel the same way, which is totally okay. So please don't take it personally if a disabled person chooses not to engage. If a child wonders how my wheelchair works, I'm more than happy to give a demo. If they ask what's "wrong" with my legs, I'll share that I was born with something called a disability. That's generally all it takes to satisfy a kid's curiosity and hopefully teach them something in a friendly way.

I don't presume to have the authority to tell someone how to parent or care for the child in their charge, but I do have some suggestions on how best to handle situations like these to make things less awkward, for kids both with and without disabilities.

And I don't just speak from the perspective of a disabled person. I've also been the mortified adult in charge. When *Frozen 2* came out, my family took our eight-year-old neighbor to see it. We handed our tickets to the ticket-taker, a gentleman with a facial difference who has worked at our local movie theater for quite some time. My young neighbor looked at him as she handed him her ticket and blurted out "What happened to your face?" I almost dropped my popcorn. But the gentleman taking the ticket answered the question with dignity and grace. I resisted the urge to scold my neighbor, instead guiding her to thank the ticket-taker for answering her question. As we headed to the theater, I grappled with what to say. I guess I'd subconsciously assumed that since my neighbor was so familiar with my mother and me using wheelchairs, she'd be just as comfortable with other physical differences. It was a valuable lesson for us both. I tried to explain that no one looks the same and that it's one of the things that makes the world such a beautiful place. I tried to tell her that it's okay to be curious, but it's not nice to just shout out questions. Honestly, I struggled to find the right words. But she seemed to understand, in her own eight-year-old way, that difference isn't a bad thing.

Did I handle this as well as I could have? Did I get through to my neighbor? I truly don't know, but I hope so. Moments like these are hard, and you never know what curveball a kid will throw. But based on experience, here's the best advice I've got: Please don't scold or shush a child for being rude. I get that this can be an instinct based on a parenting or caregiving style, but I believe these responses to a child's questions stem from the adult's shame or embarrassment around disability. If it's clear that the disabled person your kid is curious about isn't comfortable engaging, the next best thing is to respond instead of ignoring the question or yelling. So if the child sees a disabled person and says something like "Why does he walk funny?," answer as honestly as you can. "I don't know exactly why he walks the way he does, but it's likely that he has something called a disability that affects his legs. It's okay to be curious, but remember, it's not nice to say that someone who walks differently than you is walking 'funny.'"

And whatever you do, don't make a joke or mean comment in response to a child's question. A kid once asked, "Mommy, what happened to her?" and the mother replied by yanking him out of my path while saying, "You can't ask things like that; these people will run you over." Kids learn what they live, and they'll mimic what they experience. When adults model stigma and discrimination or shame and ignorance, they're perpetuating it into the attitudes and actions of future generations. Keep in mind that this applies to parents and caregivers of disabled kids too.

In search of advice on what to do when a disabled child in one's care is subjected to questions and comments, I went to my most trusted source: my parents. Weighing his words carefully, my dad pointed out that it's important to consider the context of every situation. "There are no hard-and-fast rules," he said. "Your instinct as a parent might be to want to take the opportunity to educate, especially if it's a child who said something. You'll want to defuse the awkward situation. And if a child is scolded or the adult in charge gives a harmful response, your urge might be to correct it. But also recognize that your response might not be well received. So it's best to decide on a case-by-case basis when to let it go and when it might actually be a teachable moment." My mom agreed. Thinking back on raising me, she recalled, "Dad and I wanted to help you understand that, yes, you have a disability and, yes, people are going to ask questions or treat you differently, because that's reality, unfortunately. It was important for us to make sure you knew that you shouldn't be ashamed of yourself, to teach you how you could respond in the moment, and to support you unconditionally."

Stopping the Cycle of Poor Disability Etiquette

At this point you might be worrying, *Have I said or done things to perpetuate ableism? Is my etiquette inappropriate? Can I fix this?!*

In answer to the first question, yes, you've most likely made an ableist etiquette faux pas, or several. But let's pause for a moment and take a deep breath. I have no interest in making anyone feel bad, embarrassed, or guilty. That said, I'm not just giving out free passes for ableist behavior, either. Instead, I'm encouraging you to take this chance to do better by moving forward. How? If you realize right away you've been ableist, you can try to back up and address it. If someone else points it out to you in the moment, it can be easy to feel defensive, to respond with something like "Aren't you being a little sensitive?" or "Come on, you know I didn't mean that." But the best way to respond is by genuinely taking into account how you made the other person feel.

This might be challenging if it was a passing interaction, although my mom did once have a stranger apologize for making a comment about her wheelchair. She was waiting in a long line at a store, and the woman behind her said, "You're so lucky you don't have to stand in this line." My mom just sighed and paid for her things. As she was leaving, the woman behind her wished her a nice day and added, "Hey, I really shouldn't have said that. I'm sorry." Short, simple, and self-aware.

If you know the person toward whom you've been ableist, there are more options for handling the situation in the moment. First, try not to jump to being defensive. Then consider what happened. Was it something you said or did, like making a joke that was in poor taste? Or was it something you *didn't* say or do, like not inviting a disabled friend to a party because the venue wasn't accessible? Then you can acknowledge it and genuinely apologize. Sometimes it's best to move on from there rather than prolong the conversation. But if the other person indicates that they're open to talking about it further, you can take the time to communicate, to understand how you've made the other person feel, and to figure out how you can move forward.

And if you're reflecting on something ableist you've said or done in the past that really sticks out to you, consider how you can make amends. I don't mean that you should start being overly nice to random disabled people to rebalance your karma. Nor do I recommend digging up someone else's past hurt for your own benefit. But in some cases, a thoughtful conversation can be a way to grow and better understand the disabled person's perspective—and for the person you've been ableist toward, it may be salve to a wound.

Calling Out and Calling In Ableism

Chances are you've witnessed ableism and weren't exactly sure what to do. I've been there countless times, and it can be pretty unsettling. Over time, I've learned to be kind yet straightforward. While I totally understand it's frustrating to feel as though you have to manage other people's feelings when *they're* the ones who said or did something harmful, this has been the most effective approach for me to get through to people. So let's discuss how I suggest handling some common scenarios.

It still catches me off guard when ableist language is casually thrown into a one-on-one or small group conversation, usually by people who aren't aware of the implications of what they're saying. I used to have an entire internal monologue with myself about whether I should point it out or let it go, and by the time I'd worked up the nerve to say anything, I'd feel like the moment had passed. Now I'll let the person finish what they're saying and then respond with something such as, "I'm sure you didn't have any bad intentions here, but I just wanted to let you know that [word or phrase the person said] was actually pretty discriminatory toward disabled people, and that's not okay. If you meant [non-ableist alternative], why not just say that next time?" This approach is gentle enough that it generally doesn't put people on the defensive but firm enough that they get the point.

There have been plenty of cases in which I've decided that a public call-out in the moment won't be as effective, or it might be more challenging to navigate, or it's simply not possible. For instance, if someone says or does something generally ableist in a public space or in front of a larger group (including on social media), especially if it's more complex than using an ableist word or phrase, I'll follow up privately—often referred to as calling a person *in*, rather than calling them *out*. If it's someone I know, I'm usually comfortable sending a message or making a phone call to say, "Hey, I wanted to touch base with you about something I noticed that concerned me. Is now a good time?" If it's someone I don't know, I'll send a polite but direct email laying out my concerns and offering to have a more in-depth discussion.

Things get trickier when you witness ableism directed at a specific person. Should you jump in as a defender to be a "good" ally? Should you let the person it's directed at handle it on their own so you don't come across as trying to be some kind of savior? But then, are you a "bad" ally if you don't jump in? I wish I had concrete answers for you, but it really depends on the situation. My best advice is to (1) take cues from the person experiencing the ableism, and (2) assess whether you actually have something helpful to contribute. For instance, before inserting yourself into a conversation thread on social media, consider if you're adding fuel to an ableism fire by jumping on a call-out bandwagon, or if you have a comment to add that might genuinely help put the fire out. In person, if someone you're with is subjected to ableism, it's usually best to let them lead and then echo or support as best you can. Of course, if someone appears to be in a potentially dangerous ableist situation, like an outright threat to their safety because of bullying or physical harm, definitely consider stepping in if you have the capacity and feel safe to do so.

Remember, every situation is different and you might not always get it right when it comes to pushing back against ableism. But by being more aware of the impact of your actions and the actions of others, we can all help make the world a better, less ableist place.

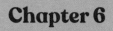

Chapter 6

Disability in the Media

Indeed, the history of disabled people in the Western world is in part the history of being on display, of being visually conspicuous while being politically and socially erased.

— Rosemarie Garland-Thomson, professor of English and bioethics

Hop into my time machine and let's go back to the early 1970s.
Ellen, the young girl who would later become my mom, was flip-
ping through *TV Guide* when she came across an ad for the kids'
show *Zoom* that stopped her in her tracks. A girl named Dee was
going to guest star on the show—and Dee had Larsen syndrome!
My mom was stunned. She'd never seen or heard about anyone
other than her brother who had the same disability—especially
not on television. Excitedly, she reached out to the station produc-
ing the show, asking to be put in touch with Dee. For a while, my
mom and Dee exchanged letters, and now, all these years later,
they're friends on Facebook. Watching Dee on an episode of *Zoom*
remained the only time during my mom's childhood that she ever
saw someone like her in the media.

    Things were just starting to change in the media landscape
by the time I was born in the 1990s. I can barely recall seeing kids
like me in books or on TV when I was a child; there are only two
examples that really stand out in my mind. The first was a picture
book about two kids in physical therapy, *Patrick and Emma Lou*,
that my mom learned about in a magazine for parents of disabled kids. I'd always smile toward the end when Patrick got sad

about his disability and Emma Lou reminded him, "You're just you, Patrick, and I'm just me." The other strong memory I have of seeing someone like me is watching Tarah Schaeffer, a little girl using a wheelchair, on *Sesame Street*. And in a twist of fate, years after the first time I saw Tarah in an episode, I had the opportunity to do for other kids what she did for me. At age ten, I appeared on multiple episodes of *Sesame Street* to educate about my life with a physical disability. And, yes, I did hang out with Elmo and Big Bird and Oscar the Grouch. Yes, it is one of the highlights of my life. I was even recognized a few times while out and about, which made me feel as though I had made an impact. But more to the point, this experience taught me at an early age about the value of positive, authentic disability representation in the media.

Truly good representations of disability in any form of media can be hard to come by. There are many common ways disability is depicted in media that reduce disabled people to one-note caricatures rather than portraying them as multidimensional human beings. Even more striking is the fact that people with disabilities often aren't represented *at all* in the media, let alone accurately and authentically. According to GLAAD's 2019–2020 "Where We Are on TV" report, which looked at 879 series regulars on broadcast programming, only 3.1 percent—just twenty-seven characters—were people with disabilities. This is nowhere close to being representative of the 15 percent of the world's population who are disabled. And if disabled people are shown, far too often it is with a complete lack of acknowledgment that we're an incredibly diverse group. In so many cases, the media has a go-to token representative of the concept of disability meant to signal "Hey, look: diversity!"—a white, straight, cisgender person with a visible physical disability, usually sitting in a wheelchair. But that's not diversity; that's just trying to check a box for representation while entirely erasing the distinctiveness within the community. Keah Brown calls this out best in her book *The Pretty One*: "There is nothing inherently wrong about telling the stories of the white and male wheelchair users—their stories are important—but there are also other stories worth telling."

And then there's the issue of media makers relying heavily on stereotypes and stigmas that reflect and perpetuate society's negative views of disability. When we're constantly surrounded by ableist depictions of disability, it's all too easy for both non-disabled and disabled people to believe it as truth. A single scene in a movie, page in a book, or article online can manipulate where the line falls between our understanding of what's inaccurate and what's reality, feeding into a harmful cycle of discrimination. And disabled people get caught right in the middle of that cycle, because the media affects not only how we're treated but also how we perceive ourselves.

So how can we break this cycle? The most powerful place to begin is to learn about what kinds of stereotypes to look for, as well as how to interpret them. The list is long, to be sure. We're going to cover some (though not all) of the ones that are most commonly used, known as media "tropes," so that you'll be better equipped to spot the difference between positive and harmful representations of disability. Please remember that the tropes we'll talk about don't each exist in a vacuum; they quite frequently intertwine and overlap within a media landscape that, for the most part, still has a ways to go in figuring out how to accurately portray disability.

Inspiration Porn

Porn. Got your attention? Popularized by the late disability activist Stella Young (who was a total badass with a knack for telling it like it is), the term *inspiration porn* is a head-turner, for sure, but it's an accurate way to describe the concept of how disabled people and their stories are objectified by the media to make observers feel warm and fuzzy or better about themselves. If you've seen a news story about a paralyzed person who trained to walk across the stage at graduation; or shared a meme showing a wheelchair user exercising, captioned "What's your excuse?"; or read a book about a character who miraculously "overcomes" their disability against all odds, then you know what I'm talking about.

Many nondisabled people get defensive when disabled people talk about inspiration porn. *What's so terrible about finding disabled people inspirational? It's just a nice story.* Well, let's dig into why someone might be so inspired by such a story. Young said it best in her TEDx talk: "We've been sold the lie that disability is a Bad Thing, capital *B*, capital *T*. It's a bad thing, and to live with a disability makes you exceptional. It's not a bad thing, and it doesn't make you exceptional." So if you buy into that lie we've been sold, then your feelings aren't really coming from a place of genuine inspiration; they're about pity, which is a patronizing way to think about people with disabilities. Those feeling are based on notions such as *Wow, at least my life isn't* that *bad* and *If those poor souls can exist in their condition, imagine what* I'm *capable of doing.* And the media capitalizes on these sentiments by creating content—news, movies, books, TV shows—that relies on "inspiring" stories of disability because people eat it up.

I'm confident that even if you've never considered the idea of inspiration porn until just now, you're familiar with what I'm talking about. In fact, I'd willingly bet that you've come across it and you've likely read or watched it. In some cases, you might have shared it, and you've possibly even sniffled into a tissue or two over it. Inspiration porn is prejudice toward disabled people that's engineered to tug at heartstrings, to be accompanied by swelling music, to be retweeted by celebrities, to be featured as the puff piece at the end of the nightly news. It's absolutely everywhere. We can break it down into a few different types.

Overcoming Adversity

Imagine a photo of a person with a prosthetic leg running on a track, paired with text that says something like, "Your excuse is invalid" or "The only disability is a bad attitude." There are countless variations of this type of inspiration porn, commonly seen in memes meant to give people a motivational push or to make them feel guilty for not appreciating all that they're capable of doing. Passive viewers of such memes might take them to mean "anything is possible," but as Stella Young pointed out in her TED talk, this is false logic. "No amount of smiling at a flight of stairs has ever made it turn into a ramp. Never," Young stated. "Smiling at a television screen isn't going to make closed captions appear for people who are deaf. No amount of standing in the middle of a bookshop and radiating a positive attitude is going to turn all those books into Braille. It's just not going to happen." And yet, many people are convinced that disability is an internal barrier that can be overcome if one only tries hard enough. There's a lack of recognition that the adversity disabled people experience has nothing to do with needing to try harder or adjusting our attitudes to be more positive. Rather, it stems from the belief that disability is some kind of personal failing.

Life's Moments

Generally, events such as weddings and graduations are personal moments that don't go viral; but if you add in the idea of over-coming disability, you're practically guaranteed millions of views from strangers. A video of a paralyzed person getting out of a wheelchair for the first dance at their wedding reception will melt people into a puddle. A video of a person with Down syndrome getting a high school diploma brings tears to people's eyes. Why? Because of a deeply held stigmatizing belief that disability holds people back from a full life. Granted, the idea of what a "full life" looks like can be, in and of itself, a pretty rigid concept based in ableist ideas of what's normal. But many, many disabled peo-ple can and do reach various life milestones, and it shouldn't be sensationalized.

I should note that I get plenty of pushback from disabled and nondisabled people alike for critiquing this kind of inspiration porn. They think I'm being rude by attacking a happy moment or assume that I begrudge another person's triumph because I must be unhappy with who I am. This couldn't be further from the truth. I believe in celebrating good things and big accomplishments. But the trouble with these kinds of stories is that they wouldn't be newsworthy at all if a disabled person wasn't the subject, and if we didn't live in a world so consumed by the ableist idea that if disabled people achieve anything, it can only be in spite of our disabilities.

Great Expectations

There's an interesting contradiction that regularly surfaces in media showing disabled people: we're held to either very high or very low expectations. For example, you might be scrolling through social media and come across an article with a headline such as "Inspiring Differently Abled Man Overcomes Odds and Climbs Mountain." On the flip side, you might find an article with a headline reading "Disabled Girl Takes Last Place in Race but Inspires Everyone." The tug-of-war between these concepts can get confusing because it feels as if there's no middle ground. If we're not finding ways to push past our disabilities and publicly demonstrating that we can leap tall buildings in a single bound, our lives must be tragic and deserving of pity (another trope that we'll get to in a moment). Both of these extremes are judgments on the worth of a disabled person, but neither acknowledges that disabled people are complex human beings like everyone else.

The media constantly perpetuates this idea of superhuman versus subhuman, and it's a total confidence drain for disabled people. Consider this. My mom once found herself feeling completely inadequate after watching a news story about an initiative for injured veterans to scale the world's highest mountains. As we discussed the story, we couldn't help wondering if we were nothing but a couple of disabled failures, sitting in our living room talking about disability representation on the news instead of climbing a massive mountain. Are we not doing enough to prove ourselves to society? Of course, the answer to this is a resounding no. We don't need to prove anything to anyone. We, like all other people, disabled or not, are both capable and fallible, with many rocky layers in between.

Not Your Good Deed

Nondisabled people are all too often painted by the media as magnanimous, saintly souls for treating disabled people with kindness. While stories such as these can be found in the media year-round, look out for prime examples of them during homecoming and prom seasons. Take this real headline: "Teens Crown Disabled Girl Homecoming Queen & Warm Our Hearts." Or this one: "Grab Your Tissues Before You Watch This Groom's Wedding Vows to His Wheelchair-Bound Bride." These kinds of stories are designed to get people to click and feel momentarily good about humanity. But, really, wouldn't you feel better if the world we lived in was inclusive? If simply being nice to a disabled person (who should be treated as a person like anyone else) *wasn't* considered newsworthy? If loving someone disabled wasn't seen as heroic? (Because it isn't!) This is an assumption my family encounters on a regular basis. People see my able-bodied dad helping two "damsels" in wheelchairs and fawn over him. He's actually been called Saint Marc, which people consider a compliment. But saying such things totally discounts all the ways my mom and I help my dad, while also asserting that his worth lies mainly in being a caregiver. Yes, he must go above and beyond the typical responsibilities of a father and husband at times, but that's not all that defines him. There are a million other reasons why he's a regular ol' great guy (and occasional grump) that have nothing to do with loving or caring for disabled family members.

Sometimes, nondisabled people are so convinced that kindness toward a disabled person is saintly that they'll go out of their way to film it happening. Contemplate this headline: "This Video of a Young Girl Playing with a Boy with Autism Will Leave You in Tears." And this one: "Restaurant Employee Feeds Disabled Customer in Random Act of Kindness." First of all, someone taking a video of a disabled person on the receiving end of kindness and sharing it should raise major red flags for you, and it happens more often than you think (generally without the consent of the disabled person). But the larger issues at play here are the beliefs that (1) helping a person with a disability is a moment worthy of recording, and (2) this private moment belongs on the news, with the focus on glorifying the nondisabled person for being a good person or doing a good deed. Such acts of kindness are perceived as an act of charity toward the poor disabled person who the world believes just needed someone to be nice to them. When moments such as these are celebrated as human-interest fodder or used to try to guilt people into being nicer, it really isn't kindness anymore.

Inspired to Make Change?

Here's the overarching problem with inspiration porn: A person can read or watch it, enjoy the quick hit of warm fuzzy feelings, click the "Share" button, and go on with their day. It's an easy way to feel good about oneself while actually perpetuating stereotypes. So when you come across media that involves a disabled person,

instead of falling for the trap, pause for a moment and ask yourself *Is this a positive representation of disability that humanizes
disabled people, or does this media just use disability to play to
emotions? Am I inspired because someone with a disability actually
did something truly inspiring, or does this feeling stem from ableist
ideas about disabled people?* If your answer in each case is the
latter, try to avoid clicking. Don't share—or maybe do share, but call
it out. This is how we start to shift attitudes and make real change.

Pity Porn

Although inspiration and tragedy are concepts that seem to be at
odds, the idea of disability as tragic stems from the same roots as
inspiration porn: pity. You might even call it "pity porn."

The "Tragedy" of Physical Disability

It's incredibly common for the media to portray disability as an
unthinkable tragedy—one of the worst fates to befall not only
the disabled person but also the nondisabled people in their life.
Depending on your age, you might remember seeing what many
disabled people revile as one of the most glaring examples of the
tragedy trope: the annual Labor Day telethon for the Muscular
Dystrophy Association (MDA) hosted by comedian Jerry Lewis.
From 1966 to 2010, Lewis made it his business to tug at the heartstrings and wallets of viewers to raise money for the MDA to work
on research for a cure. The children with muscular dystrophy who
appeared on the telethons were called "Jerry's Kids." He portrayed
them as pathetic charity cases, even going so far, in an article he

wrote, as to refer to them as "half a person." (Despite this fraught, ableist history, and vigorous protest from disability activists, the MDA chose to revive the telethon in 2020.)

Perhaps the most common expressions of the tragedy mindset are the sorrowful responses upon learning someone's baby has been born with a disability, or when someone has been permanently injured or received a disability diagnosis. Again, disability is believed to be a "bad thing" for those who experience it and for those who are part of a disabled person's life. In many films and television shows, the "tragedy" of disability serves as a plot point in the development of a nondisabled character. One of the most recognizable examples of this occurrence is the character of Tiny Tim in Charles Dickens's *A Christmas Carol.* The sweet but pitiful, sickly little boy's circumstances ultimately teach Ebenezer Scrooge to quit being such a heartless miser. The story is supposed to warm hearts, but the stereotyping leaves me cold.

Tiny Tim and the stereotype of the tragic disabled person aren't going anywhere, though. Nearly two centuries after the publication of Dickens's novel, writers and media makers are still singing the same old tune. One of the worst recent offenders is Jojo Moyes's bestselling book-club favorite (that became a girls' night tearjerker film), *Me Before You.* Moyes paints Will, one of the main characters, as a successful and happy nondisabled man, but after becoming paralyzed he becomes convinced his life will be nothing but misery. Despite a blossoming romance with his caregiver, Louisa, Will remains fixated on the idea that he is a burden to himself and those around him. Spoiler alert: Rather than continue to live and adapt to life as a disabled man, Will chooses assisted suicide. The message? Disability is a fate worse than death. Sadly, the millions of fans of the book and movie don't see it this way. They see a love story in which Will is noble for choosing death to free Louisa from being trapped in a future with him, and they see those who critique the exploitation of disability as a tragic plot device as bitter cynics. We're not bitter, though; we just have the audacity to believe that disabled lives are worth living.

Stigmatizing Mental Illness

As with physical and intellectual disabilities, media portrayals of mental illness are often problematic and woefully mishandled. As writer s.e. smith, who identifies as mentally ill, wrote in an essay for Disability in Kidlit:

> Mental illness is frequently dealt with in very troped, and often harmful, ways, illustrating that creators didn't take the time to research, learn about the lived experiences of the communities they are writing about, or think about the responsibility involved in depicting mentally ill people, an already marginalised group within our larger culture.

Think about the popularity of tabloid stories with headlines such as "You Won't Believe Which Celeb Is Having a Massive Mental Breakdown!" Our culture encourages us to make light of these very real experiences while we toss popcorn into our mouths, treating human beings as nothing more than a "hot mess" at which we can gawk. Media coverage of Britney Spears is a prime, highly visible example of this. Her mental health has, at various times throughout her career, been memed, mocked, and exploited—put on display for all to watch and judge. We are quick to forget humanity for the sake of our own entertainment, especially when it comes to mental illness.

Conversely, mental illness is also frequently presented not as light gossip but as dangerous and scary. It's common for media discussions about perpetrators of mass violence to throw around terms such as "mentally ill" or "crazy" or "insane." But the association of violence with mental illness is largely a harmful myth, which studies have debunked. In fact, these studies have shown that people with mental illness are more likely to be victims of violence than perpetrators. The inclination to scapegoat mental illness is really just an ableist way to derail the conversations that need to be had about putting an end to mass violence.

Freaks and Other "Abnormalities"

We live in a society that, by glorifying and trying to "cash in," perpetuates the harm of ogling and/or mocking people who look, sound, communicate, or behave outside arbitrary norms. Even though it may often seem like harmless amusement or entertainment, this kind of objectification of people who look "different" has deep historical roots in the perception of visibly disabled people as "freaks." Since the earliest days of recorded history, explains Leonard Cassuto in the book *Keywords for Disability Studies*, "Human oddities, whether alive, dead, or stillborn, were confined (often against their will) and categorized through theatrical display." Such displays were, as mentioned in chapter 3, turned into moneymaking schemes by inviting the public to jeer at "freaks" in person during freak shows. These days, all a person needs to do to witness modern-day freak shows is turn on the television or scroll through social media. Take nonfiction "medical mystery" series, or fictional medical dramas such as *Grey's Anatomy*. Shows of this nature dramatize stories of people with complex diagnoses, often playing up visible physical anomalies. The creators of these programs know what most viewers want—the "weirder," the better. And while these types of series can occasionally be educational, they usually rely on society's morbid fascination with minds and bodies that are "different." Unfortunately, shows such as these end up reinforcing stigma, creating a gateway for fascination to escalate very quickly to cruelty. To you, a medical drama might be a good binge watch for a Friday night. But real disabled people are harmed by the stereotypes that are perpetuated, because they can carry over into real-world interactions.

Melissa Blake, a prolific writer and advocate who has a genetic physical disability called Freeman-Sheldon syndrome, knows this all too well. "My decision to be so visible and so open about my life and my disability has, indeed, shown me quite a nasty side of people," Blake reflects. "I've lost count of the number of times people have mocked my appearance. These trolls never offer a critique of what I've written; they always go for the insults about my looks. We live in such an appearance-focused society, so if you don't look a certain way, the trolls pounce on that." But Blake, fabulous human that she is, has been pushing back by bringing positive disability representation into the world with her own spin on it. "Their words hurt," she says, "but they've actually motivated me. To be more vocal. To speak up. And, yes, to show my face (hi, selfies!) any chance I get. I may not be able to change everyone's point of view, but I'm determined to show the world that disabled people are here and we're not going anywhere!"

Sex and Relationships

Aren't able to. Don't want to. Shouldn't. These are the assumptions that many people make about disabled people finding love and having sex. In fact, disability, romance, and sexuality are seen as being so completely at odds that most mainstream media avoids even the slightest implication that these things can be associated. From media to medicine, there's a pretty big lack of information and representation, not to mention a lot of *mis*representation. Disabled people are far too often considered childlike, breakable, undesirable, damaged goods who are unfit to be sexually active or sexualized—and if we are, there's an assumption it's okay only in a weird, taboo way. Indeed, there are parts of the internet where disabled people are not only sexualized but actively fetishized by people known as "devotees," but that's a story for another book. Anyway, allow me to squash the assumptions that disabled people can't be sexy or sexual! We can and do exist on the same spectrum of sexual preferences and identities as nondisabled people, and we can have active, healthy sex lives. Some disabled people are cisgender and heterosexual, and others identify as lesbian, gay, bisexual, trans, queer, intersex, or asexual (LGBTQIA+). Some disabled people aren't interested in sex at all, and others have high sex drives. Some disabled people are into kink, and others prefer things a little less spicy. We, like everyone else, contain romantic and sexual multitudes.

Don't get me wrong; media portrayals of disabled people having sex or being objects of sexual attraction do exist. But they're still few and very far between when you consider just how overtly sexual the media actually is. How many visibly disabled people have you come across in lingerie ads? Cologne ads? Subtly suggestive storylines? Hot and heavy sex scenes? Perhaps a few, but it's still pretty uncommon. Sexualization and objectification can be problematic, but when it comes to the disability community, we often have to push for even the bare minimum of acknowledgment that we, too, can be sexual beings.

We're currently still at a point in which disabled love and sex is human interest fodder rather than a fact of life. For example, the Netflix series *Love on the Spectrum* is a reality television-esque show allowing viewers a voyeuristic look into the romantic lives of Autistic people. So many viewers absolutely ate it up, finding it heartwarming and moving to watch Autistic people navigating relationships. But many Autistic people weren't quite so enthused. When I spoke to autistic attorney and activist Haley Moss, she said, "I think what's problematic about the show is it views autistic people solely through a neurotypical gaze—what people want to assume and believe autistics are all about. We're just as human as anyone else (which the show tries to capture); it just ignores a lot of aspects of who we are." As it happens, this is a pretty common issue that arises in media about disability. Disabled people are portrayed as oddities for being who they are and pushed to fit into molds of what's considered "normal." But this can change. How? In an article for *Cosmopolitan UK*, Marianne Eloise, who identifies as autistic, reflected: "What *Love on the Spectrum* has shown autistic people need, more than anything, is the opportunity to tell our own stories, to not be observed and fetishised." Indeed, this is what the disability community as a whole requires to truly shift how the world sees us.

Positive Portrayals

We've talked so much about negative portrayals of disability, it's about time I reassure you that good disability representation absolutely does exist. You just have to know what to look for, so I'll give you a big hint: Authenticity. People with disabilities know ourselves and our experiences best, and we use them to breathe life into stories both real and imagined. We've always been out here creating the kind of representation that's so often missing from the mainstream because of the nondisabled gatekeepers who decide whose stories should be told. But bit by bit, the mainstream is letting us in, slowly centering the lived experiences of people with all kinds of disabilities. We have much further to go in truly representing the depth and breadth of diversity within the disability community, but we are moving in the right direction.

Remember, media can be a mixed bag, with positive and negative aspects of disability representation frequently coexisting. Sometimes a story that refers to people with disabilities as having "special needs" might make a valid point about inaccessibility or ableism. Or a movie with a cringeworthy, inspiration porn storyline has a moment that feels true to the reality of the disability experience. Small victories in representation are important.

There are many bigger victories too. As a physically disabled person, I feel understood when I watch TV shows such as *Special*, a Netflix series written by and starring Ryan O'Connell, who has cerebral palsy. The deep sense of familiarity watching him navigate life in a disabled body is a breath of fresh air for me. And for nondisabled people, the show is an entry point into understanding disability as a part of the human experience.

I feel so much joy when I see a person in a wheelchair in an advertisement and learn that they're actually a wheelchair user in real life. I'm far from the only one. When Ulta Beauty featured wheelchair-user Steph Aiello in an ad for its store, a photo of a young girl named Maren, also a wheelchair user, staring up at the poster in awe, went viral. How I wish I had experienced something like that when I was little.

And I love watching disabled models strut their stuff. I mean, have you seen Aaron Philip? She's a Black transgender model who has cerebral palsy who's worked with major brands such as Dove and Sephora. Madeline Stuart? She's a model with Down syndrome who's been on Fashion Week runways from New York to Paris. Jillian Mercado? She's a Latinx model with muscular dystrophy who's modeled for Beyoncé's merchandise line! And how about Nyle DiMarco? He's a (ridiculously hot) deaf activist and actor who won *America's Next Top Model* in 2015. Yes, I recognize that there's largely still an overarching theme of conventional attractiveness that's acceptable in the modeling industry, even for disabled people, but I'm all about incremental progress.

Rather than nondisabled people pretending to be disabled or imagining our experiences, let's aim for a world in which disabled people are fixtures in every part of the media industry, so stories *about* us are meaningfully told *by* us. There might be box-office power in having a major nondisabled celebrity pretend to be disabled for a role in a film but, in so many ways, there's more power in having actual disabled people shape media that involves disability. Angel Giuffria, an actor with a limb difference, shared with me that she believes "at this point in time, where there is such a discrepancy in representation of people with and without disabilities in the media, it's doing a true disservice to the audience to not see accurate or genuine representation or depiction of people with disabilities in daily life." She's hopeful we'll reach a point where the media is fully representative of all types of humans.

"I think at that point," Giuffria continues, "we no longer have to worry about who's playing what or whom because it will be truthful and genuine. But right now is not that time. I think until we get to that point, we need to continue to work toward having disabled actors play disabled characters." We need more characters with disabilities on screen and on stage played by disabled actors; more books with disabled characters written by disabled people; more disabled models in advertising; more and better disability representation, period.

Actor Ryan J. Haddad, who has cerebral palsy, agrees. In an interview with me, he shared:

> Lived experience trumps any sort of research that one can do about what it is to be disabled. We have perspective as people who live disabled lives that no writers who aren't disabled, no directors who aren't disabled, no producers who aren't disabled can impart to an actor who isn't disabled. If a character is disabled and I'm disabled, all I'm thinking about is how to intentionally bring truth to the words and actions of that character. I don't have to think about putting on disability because I just am. There's this barrier between a nondisabled actor and a disabled character that can't really be penetrated, though Hollywood would have you believe otherwise and gives awards to people who seemingly masterfully portray disability just because they were able to do all those things at once."

It's true. People love to ooh and ah over nondisabled people conjuring an illusion of disability, but that's not true inclusion. It's just a way to sell more tickets.

In an ideal media landscape, we'd reach a point in which disability representation by disabled people is the rule rather than the exception, and wouldn't be noteworthy at all. And beyond that, disabled people wouldn't be pigeonholed into only disability-focused media. "We need to better integrate actors with disabilities into all roles," Giuffria urges, "by opening up casting parameters and giving disabled actors the opportunity to audition for more than roles purely about disability." This would truly be the pinnacle of positive, authentic disability representation—to be surrounded by media that actually reflects and celebrates disability as part of humanity.

Conclusion:
Calling All Allies and Accomplices

I'm really glad that we stuck together through this learning process, but here's the thing—the process isn't over. Neither of us is an expert on disability simply because we made it to the end of this book. Although I included perspectives from other people throughout, ultimately this book remains one woman's take on disability. There's no way to become a master of such diverse human experience, but we can and should keep learning. And we can apply that learning by taking meaningful action, otherwise known as "allyship."

Ally is one of those buzzwords that gets thrown around a lot, frequently among well-meaning people who want to be supportive of marginalized communities. Obviously, this is super-important, but it's even more important to remember that "ally" isn't an official label or title. Simply saying "I'm an ally to the XYZ-marginalized community" isn't how allyship works. In fact, being an ally is really more of a "show, don't tell" kind of thing. But how can we show allyship?

First, let's reflect on your reasoning and motivation for wanting to be an ally to disabled people. Is it because you feel pity toward people with disabilities? I'm hoping that after reading this book, you recognize that feeling that way is pretty condescending. Do you perhaps feel guilty for having some form of nondisabled privilege that people in the disability community don't share, so you want to make up for it? Sorry to burst your bubble, but that's more about self-interest than solidarity. Are you feeling altruistic and want to help? You're moving in the right direction, but let's pause for a moment.

While talking with me about the deeper meaning of allyship, Autistic activist Reyma McCoy McDeid dropped a hard-hitting question. "If you do not belong to a particular marginalized community and you want to help that community, why do you associate the word 'help' with that community?" she begins. "That really needs to be unpacked before you approach that community." Really good question. If I had to venture a guess, I'd say it has a whole lot to do with the fact that both helplessness and being in need of help are two of the overarching stereotypes associated with disability. This means that the first step to being an ally is unlearning this misconception and recognizing that disabled people aren't in need of saving. We're in need of a world that recognizes our rights and our humanity without question.

McCoy McDeid emphasizes that this will happen only if we look beyond the standard definition of allyship. "To be an ally is to help people who are marginalized in some capacity to make the most of their life in this unchanged system," she says. "To be an accomplice, on the other hand, is to work side by side with people who are marginalized, to confront the system and contribute to shifting it accordingly." Technically, the definition of *accomplice* has to do with committing acts of wrongdoing, but in this context, we're talking about committing to change.

Whether you call it being an ally or an accomplice, you can be a part of making change happen. Here's how.

Think of Allyship as a Journey, Not a Destination

I believe acknowledging the process of allyship, and not the end result, is a helpful way to empower it. Let's consider a concrete example of this to start. Say you've decided to work on eliminating ableist words from your vocabulary and helping others realize why they shouldn't use them (really solid goals, by the way). Some days you might catch yourself before a word slips out; other days you might say something or hear someone else say something ableist and not even realize it. And on still other days, you might say something ableist or hear someone else do it and realize it immediately. Stopping or correcting yourself or another person is important, but it isn't a free pass to pat yourself on the back and say, "I was a good ally today." Ableist words are so embedded in society's vocabulary and mindset that avoiding them and actively remembering to use alternatives needs to be an ongoing process. To apply this idea more broadly to dismantling ableism, remember: Being an ally needs to be an ongoing process.

Nothing about Us without Us

Many in the disability community use the slogan *Nothing about us without us* as a bold reminder of the fact that we're the ones who must be in charge of every aspect of our lives. All too often, people with disabilities are relegated to the sidelines in conversations about issues that directly affect us—everything from individual circumstances to major policy decisions. I'd say this is due to an assumption that we can't communicate and advocate for ourselves, but it often goes beyond that. In far too many situations, it doesn't seem to occur to nondisabled people that disabled people can and do have our own thoughts, viewpoints, and opinions. Journalists interview parents and "specialists" about us instead of coming directly to us. Doctors and teachers talk to caregivers about us instead of talking to us. Policymakers consult nondisabled "experts" about us instead of consulting us. You get the idea. But, as always, disabled people are the experts on our own lives. So please, don't speak for us, about us, or over us. Speak to us and with us.

In the same vein, many nondisabled people deem themselves advocates "for" the disability community. Believe me, I'm all about the power of advocacy, but it's absolutely crucial to make sure that people with disabilities are leading the charge in any and all efforts. Advocate alongside us, rather than on our behalf. Stand (or sit!) in solidarity with us, rather than moving ahead of us.

Pass the Microphone

If you are in a position of privilege, rather than using that position to amplify your own voice, ask yourself whose perspectives are missing from the conversation. Then lift up and amplify the perspectives of those people who should be centered instead. This isn't necessarily just about keeping quiet and listening, though that's always a crucial part. It's often also about actively redirecting people who may be overstepping or who are ignoring the perspectives of disabled people entirely. It's about ensuring that disabled people are respectfully given the platforms, opportunities, and space to make our messages known.

We need to remember that passing the mic isn't something that only nondisabled people need to do. Disabled people aren't off the hook. All of us must recognize the ways in which we are both marginalized and privileged, and to know when to step up and when to step back. I asked author and artist Naomi Ortiz—whose poignant work focuses on Disability Justice, intersectionality, and self-care for activists—what we all need to understand about passing the mic. "[It] is not a one-time thing," she said. "It's a series of choices to build relationships, learn together, disagree without silencing the other. It's about building up our capacity to honor difference and appreciate the messiness."

Don't Try to Understand Disability by Trying It on for an Afternoon

Schools, businesses, and organizations seem to have an affinity for hosting disability "awareness" or "empathy" trainings and events, during which nondisabled participants are encouraged to participate in simulations of disability experiences. They might be asked to wear earplugs as a way to understand hearing loss, or a blindfold to understand vision loss. They might be asked to try pushing themselves around in a wheelchair or walk using crutches. Conventional wisdom may say that people learn by doing; but let me tell you, when it comes to trying to understand the experiences of people with disabilities, this is absolutely not the way to do it. A game of pretend won't help you understand a person's entire life experience and identity. In fact, simulations often have the totally opposite effect on participants, evoking feelings of pity and fear around disability.

I'll never forget the time when a resident assistant (RA) in my college dorm asked if she could borrow my wheelchair for her disability awareness event—an obstacle course she'd set up in the lounge. What was I supposed to do while she was using it? Sit stranded in my room while the other people who lived in my residence hall treated my expensive mobility equipment like a toy? I mean, don't get me wrong, life on wheels can be fun. But it's not a game. I remember feeling like less of a person in that moment. The RA didn't care about giving me a chance to educate people about my experiences or giving nondisabled people a genuine opportunity to learn about disability. It was really all about letting people get a kick out of pretending to be me for a few minutes. Needless to say, I declined her request.

So how can you learn about disability if you're not simulating it? Instead of trying it on, actively seek out the work and words of disabled people. Read books. Watch documentaries. Listen to podcasts. Invite us to give presentations. Engage in open, honest conversations with us. But please, don't pretend to be us.

Recognize, Credit, and Compensate Disabled People

We need to recognize the work of disabled people without demanding that work from them. We need to give credit and compensation where it's due. There are so many people with disabilities who take the time to be vulnerable and share their experiences to educate those around them. While it can certainly be a rewarding process to push for progress and change perceptions, the work of translating painful encounters involving discriminatory attitudes and ableist systems into broader lessons can be difficult and emotionally taxing, especially because we have to do it over and over. In most situations, I embrace opportunities to teach people about disability, but no disabled person should be expected to always be ready to explain themselves or the issues impacting their lives.

It's so important to not only directly acknowledge but also shine a spotlight on disabled people and their work. And remember, the disability community is statistically at a disproportionate socioeconomic disadvantage. So when requesting work from disabled people—a blog post, a speech, accessibility consulting, and so on—please make sure you're compensating them fairly. We need to earn a living like anyone else!

Own Up to Mistakes and Apologize When Needed

Genuine allyship is not always going to be smooth, simple, or straightforward. You might find yourself feeling unsure of how to handle certain situations. And chances are there will be missteps and mistakes in all of our futures, including mine. So, if and when that happens—you host an inaccessible event, say something ableist, make an etiquette faux pas—reflect on how you can do better. And if someone points out the mistake before you realize it on your own and asks you to take accountability, you might find yourself feeling uncomfortable. You might even find yourself feeling defensive. But instead of jumping to defend yourself, take some time to sit with how you're feeling. Ask yourself, *Should I be focusing on myself in a situation where I've hurt or caused harm to others, or should I take this as a learning opportunity to reduce hurt and harm?* I hope you'll choose the second option.

And then, if you can, take the initiative to apologize. Please don't do this just to ease your own guilt, though. Try to do it with a true openness and willingness to learn. This might not be easy, and it won't necessarily be a magic fix, but it will be a start to moving forward in a way that uplifts the disability community. On her blog, *Leaving Evidence*, Disability Justice activist Mia Mingus explains that being accountable is not just about apologizing, but about your actions that follow. "True accountability is not only apologizing, but understanding the impacts your actions have caused on yourself and others and then making amends or reparations to the harmed parties," she elaborates. "But most important, true accountability is changing your behavior so that the harm, violence, and abuse does not happen again." Always remember that accountability and allyship are ongoing efforts.

Most Important, Keep Learning

In a world where stigmatizing messages about disability come at us from every direction, I recognize that it can be more than a little challenging to unlearn long-held biases and misconceptions. I know that trying to wrap your mind around the complexities of disability is no simple task, especially because society is brimming with injustices and so much in need of change. I've definitely had moments of grappling with whether pushing ahead is worth it when ableism is so strongly and deeply interwoven into the fabric of our society. Sometimes I feel as though no matter how hard I work, it's like pushing a boulder up a hill; except the hill has steps and I'm stuck at the bottom.

I'm no motivational speaker, but now is not the time for a defeatist attitude! Whenever I start to feel that way, I remind myself that all it takes is shifting one person's perspective, changing one mind, to have a ripple effect. My hope is that this book was the start of this ripple for you, a stone thrown into an ocean of words and wisdom from the disability community. Because we all have to start somewhere in coming to an understanding of disability as part of the human experience.

Thank you for letting me be just one tiny part of your learning journey. Now, keep going.

Further Reading and Resources

When I remind people that there is no singular disability experience and then encourage them to learn more, they often ask me where to begin. The following books, films, online videos, and hashtags that I've compiled are starting points that I recommend. But don't stop here. Let these resources open doors and lead down paths to ongoing learning about disability. For a complete bibliography of the sources that I consulted in writing this book, visit www.wordsiwheelby.com/demystifying-disability-bibliography.

Books

About Us: Essays from the Disability Series of the New York Times. Edited by Peter Catapano and Rosemarie Garland-Thomson. New York: Liveright, 2019.

All the Weight of Our Dreams: On Living Racialized Autism. Edited by Lydia X. Z. Brown, E. Ashkenazy, and Morénike Giwa Onaiwu. Lincoln, NE: DragonBee Press, 2017.

Being Heumann: An Unrepentant Memoir of a Disability Rights Activist. Judith Heumann and Kristen Joiner. Boston: Beacon Press, 2020.

Black Disabled Art History 101. Leroy F. Moore Jr. Edited by Nicola A. McClung and Emily A. Nussbaum. San Francisco: Xochitl Justice Press, 2017.

Care Work: Dreaming Disability Justice. Leah Lakshmi Piepzna-Samarasinha. Vancouver: Arsenal Pulp Press, 2018.

The Collected Schizophrenias: Essays. Esmé Weijun Wang. Minneapolis: Graywolf Press, 2019.

The Color of My Mind: Mental Health Narratives from People of Color. Dior Vargas. Berkeley, CA: Reclamation Press, 2019.

Disability Visibility: First-Person Stories from the Twenty-First Century. Edited by Alice Wong. New York: Vintage Books, 2020.

Disfigured: On Fairy Tales, Disability, and Making Space. Amanda Leduc. Toronto: Coach House Books, 2020.

Don't Call Me Inspirational: A Disabled Feminist Talks Back. Harilyn Rousso. Philadelphia: Temple University Press, 2013.

Golem Girl: A Memoir. Riva Lehrer. New York: One World, 2020.

Haben: The Deafblind Woman Who Conquered Harvard Law. Haben Girma. New York: Twelve, 2019.

Hearing Happiness: Deafness Cures in History. Jaipreet Virdi. Chicago: University of Chicago Press, 2020.

Lost in a Desert World: An Autobiography. Roland Johnson. Philadelphia: Speaking for Ourselves, 1994.

Loud Hands: Autistic People, Speaking. Edited by Julia Bascom. Washington, DC: Autistic Self Advocacy Network, 2012.

My Body Politic: A Memoir. Simi Linton. Ann Arbor: University of Michigan Press, 2006.

The Pretty One: On Life, Pop Culture, Disability, and Other Reasons to Fall in Love with Me. Keah Brown. New York: Atria Books, 2019.

Say Hello. Carly Findlay. Sydney: HarperCollins Australia, 2019.

Sick: A Memoir. Porochista Khakpour. New York: Harper Perennial, 2018.

Sitting Pretty: The View from My Ordinary Resilient Disabled Body. Rebekah Taussig. New York: HarperOne, 2020.

Skin, Tooth, and Bone: The Basis of Movement Is Our People, A Disability Justice Primer. Patty Berne and Sins Invalid, 2019.

Strangers Assume My Girlfriend Is My Nurse. Shane Burcaw. New York: Roaring Brook Press, 2019.

Stutterer Interrupted: The Comedian Who Almost Didn't Happen. Nina G. Berkeley, CA: She Writes Press, 2019.

Sustaining Spirit: Self-Care for Social Justice. Naomi Ortiz. Berkeley, CA: Reclamation Press, 2018.

Too Late to Die Young: Nearly True Tales from a Life. Harriet McBryde Johnson. New York: Picador, 2006.

What Can a Body Do?: How We Meet the Built World. Sara Hendren. New York: Riverhead Books, 2020.

Films

Bottom Dollars. Directed by Jordan Melograna. Rooted in Rights, 2017.

Code of the Freaks. Directed by Salome Chasnoff. Kino Lorber, 2020.

Crip Camp: A Disability Revolution. Directed by James LeBrecht and Nicole Newnham. Higher Ground Productions, 2020.

Fixed: The Science/Fiction of Human Enhancement. Directed by Regan Brashear. Making Change Media, 2014.

Intelligent Lives. Directed by Dan Habib. LikeRightNow Films LLC, 2018.

Jeremy the Dud. Directed by Ryan Chamley. genU and Geelong's Robot Army Productions, 2017.

The Kids Are All Right. Directed by Kerry Richardson. 2005.

Lives Worth Living. Directed by Eric Neudel. Independent Television Service, 2011.

Sins Invalid: An Unshamed Claim to Beauty. Directed by Patty Berne. New Day Films, 2013.

Trust Me, I'm Sick. Arlo Pictures and Suffering the Silence. 2020.

Unrest. Directed by Jennifer Brea. Shella Films and Little by Little Films, 2017.

Who Am I to Stop It? Directed by Cheryl Green and Cynthia J. Lopez. StoryMinders and Eleusis Films, 2016.

Online Videos

"3 Ways to Make Your Content More Accessible for Disabled People." Andrea Lausell. March 31, 2020. https://youtu.be/VtMEUGM15dU.

"5 Phrases Disabled People Are Tired Of | Decoded." MTV Impact, November 2, 2018. https://youtu.be/7DSL-2hsRk8.

"Casual Ableist Language." Annie Elainey. April 5, 2016. https://youtu.be/a1rrSXkFqGE.

"Comedian Laurence Clark Demonstrates Why He Hates Being Called Inspiring." Laurence Clark. August 25, 2012. https://youtu.be/fx9fAEJeI0E.

"Dating Struggles for People with Disabilities." Sitting Pretty Lolo. October 15, 2017. https://youtu.be/LXtIWb7i0Pc.

"Disability Sensitivity Training Video." DCGovernment, October 2, 2014. https://youtu.be/Gv1aDEFlXq8.

"Don't Look Down on Me." Jonathan Novick. August 7, 2014. https://youtu.be/mD_PWU6K514.

"How I Drive from a Wheelchair!!" Roll with Cole & Charisma. January 9, 2019. https://youtu.be/8Q2gS-o1-X0.

"How To Cuddle—5 Amazing Cuddling Tips." Squirmy and Grubs. July 12, 2018. https://youtu.be/TPnotWtuSOo.

"I Got 99 Problems . . . Palsy Is Just One." Maysoon Zayid, TED. December 2013. https://www.ted.com/talks/maysoon_zayid_ i_got_99_problems_palsy_is_just_one.

"I'm Not Your Inspiration, Thank You Very Much." Stella Young, TED. April 2014. https://www.ted.com/talks/stella_young_i_m_ not_ your_inspiration_thank_you_very_much.

"In My Language." Silentmiaow. January 14, 2007. https://youtu.be/JnylM1hI2jc.

"Judy Heumann Fights for People with Disabilities." *Drunk History*, Comedy Central. February 20, 2018. http://www.cc.com/ video-clips/2p86bgdrunk-history-judy-heumann-fights-for-people-with-disabilities.

"Navigating Life as a Deaf and Hearing Couple." Chella Man. February 27, 2020. https://youtu.be/AjYz8ni1VFM.

"Zach Anner & The Quest for the Rainbow Bagel." Cerebral Palsy Foundation. March 20, 2017. https://youtu.be/LhpUJRGrZgc.

Hashtags

#AbleismExists

#AccessIsLove

#ActuallyAutistic

#BlackDisabledLivesMatter

#CripTheVote

#DisabilitySolidarity

#DisabilityTooWhite

#DisabilityTwitter

#DisabledAndCute

#DisHist

#InaccessibilityMeans

#ItsAccessibleBut

#NoBodyIsDisposable

#SuckItAbleism

#ThingsDisabledPeopleKnow

Acknowledgments

I didn't know that a late-2018 interview with writer Kelly Dawson about the added expenses of being disabled would so radically alter the course of the next few years of my life. We became fast friends, and when she invited me to join her in guest-cohosting an episode on disability for the podcast *Call Your Girlfriend*, I was honestly just thrilled to have an excuse to spend more time talking to someone as cool and totally on-point as she is. As it happens, that podcast was a springboard to this book; and for all of that, I am grateful.

Thank you to my literary agent, Laura Lee Mattingly, for believing in me enough to reach out after listening to that episode of *Call Your Girlfriend*. Without your sure, steady guidance and ability to steer me in a direction more aligned with my work than even my own initial book ideas, I can't imagine ever having started this writing journey.

Thank you to the incredible team at Ten Speed Press for bringing my manuscript to life. By the time I hung up after my first phone call with my editor, Kaitlin Ketchum, my entire being was buzzing with excitement and certainty that Ten Speed was where I wanted my book to find a home. Kaitlin, I am so truly appreciative of every nuanced edit and encouraging conversation about the complexities of disability, and of your willingness to learn and engage thoughtfully along the way. Thank you to Doug Ogan and Want Chyi for your insightful input and edits throughout the process. Thank you to Serena Sigona for gracefully managing the production of this book. And thank you to Isabelle Gioffredi, Betsy Stromberg, and Sarah Rose Weitzman for designing a book that is so truly beautiful. Thanks also to copyeditor Kristi Hein and proofreader Carolyn Keating.

Thank you to Tyler Feder for bringing my dream book cover to life with your illustrations. Your art is a true celebration of human diversity and it brings me such joy.

Thank you to every single person who so generously gave of their time to share their thoughts, ideas, and anecdotes and allowed me to feature them. While one book simply cannot encompass the wisdom of an entire community, it is because of all of you that I was able to create something that explains why the disability experience is so much bigger than the story of any one person

Thank you also to the disability community as a whole. I know the concept of community is a complicated one, but my respect for all of you is boundless. Thank you for your advocacy, your activism, and your pursuits of justice, and for being unapologetically who you are.

Thank you to my Grandma Edie; Grandma Evelyn; all of my aunts, uncles, and cousins; and my friends who cheered me on relentlessly and never stopped supporting me, even as the contents of this book remained pretty much a complete mystery to all of you as I worked on it. Please know that listing your names would take far more lines in this book than I could possibly fit, but I love you all with my whole heart.

And finally, thank you to my parents for loving me through this. I will never have exactly the right words to tell you what it means to have such a patient, unwavering, unconditional support system. Dad, thank you for every piece of practical advice as I wrote, for all the jokes and hugs to ease my moments of whining and complaining, and for always knowing how to get me to "calm down now, don't stress, take it easy." Mom, thank you for sitting with me and arguing about—I mean, carefully discussing—the manuscript line by line, comma by comma, helping to shape this book into what it has become. I love you both, Mom and Dad, more than anybody can.

About the Author

Emily Ladau is a disability rights activist, writer, and speaker whose career began at ten years old, when she appeared on *Sesame Street* to educate children about her life with a physical disability. Emily graduated with a BA in English from Adelphi University and now serves on the school's board of trustees. In 2017, she was named one of Adelphi's 10 Under 10 Young Alumni. In 2018, she was awarded the Paul G. Hearne Emerging Leader Award from the American Association of People with Disabilities.

Emily is the digital content and community manager for the Disability & Philanthropy Forum and cohosts *The Accessible Stall* podcast, a show that delves into disability issues. She also runs a business providing consultation, editorial services, and communications strategies for multiple disability-related organizations and initiatives.

Emily's writing has been published in the *New York Times*, *SELF*, *Salon*, *Vice*, and *HuffPost*, and she has served as a source for NPR, *Vox*, and the *Washington Post*. Emily has spoken before audiences across the United States, from the U.S. Department of Education to the United Nations, with a focus on disability identity, sharing our stories, and harnessing social media as tools for people to become engaged in disability and social justice issues.

More about Emily's work can be found on her website, WordsIWheelBy.com. Follow her on Twitter at @emily_ladau.

Index

A

"able-bodied," use of term, 25
ableism, 3.
    see also accessibility
being mindful of, 75–77, 76
calling out/calling in, 115–17
definition, 70
differing perspectives by
    disabled community on,
    73–74
disability etiquette and,
    114–15
elevators in subways
    systems and, 71
in everyday interactions.
    See disability etiquette
examples of, 84–85
as ingrained in our society,
    70–71
in media depictions of
    disability, 122
motives for advocating
    against, 74
sheltered workshops
    and, 72
Social Security Disability
    Insurance (SSDI) and, 50
struggles against
    internalizing, 75
words we use and, 19–20
ableist words, 143
accessibility
airlines, 55
Architectural Barriers Act
    (1968), 51
asking about someone's
    needs for, 92
elevators in subway
    systems, 71
eliminating inaccessibility
    and, 82
examples of accommoda-
    tions for, 77–78, 81

excuses for not imple-
    menting, 80
feelings and experiences
    related to inaccessibility,
    78–81
finding information and
    guidance on, 81–82
inclusivity and, 83
polling places, 55
systemic ableism and, 71
accessible amenities, non-
    disabled people
    using, 108–9
accessible parking, 11, 27,
    107, 109
accommodations, 78
accountability, 147–48
Achieving a Better Life
    Experience (ABLE) Act
    (2014), 59
acquired disabilities, 38
activism. See disability rights
    activism
ADA Education and Reform Act
    (2017), 60
ADA National Network, 81–82
Adelante Development
    Center, 72
adversity, media depiction of
    overcoming, 124–25
African Americans, intersec-
    tionality and, 33–34
Aiello, Steph, 137
Air Carrier Access Act
    (1986), 55
airlines, 55
allyship (being an ally to dis-
    abled people), 141–49
American Disabled for Atten-
    dant Programs Today
    (ADAPT), 54–55, 60
American Sign Language, 56
Americans with Disabilities Act
    (ADA), 56–58, 73

ADA Education and Reform
    Act (2017), 60
    disability defined in, 8
apologies, 15, 114–15, 148
apparent (visible)
    disabilities, 37
Architectural Barriers Act
    (1968), 51, 52
asylums, 52
autism and autistic community
    behavioral therapy and, 84
    infantilization and, 100
    in the media, 135
    neurodiversity movement
        and, 66
    stimming and, 104–5
    use of words when talking
        about, 11, 13, 25
Autistic Self Advocacy
    Network, 59

B

Barbarin, Imani, 9, 76
Barrows, Max, 65
Bascom, Julia, 100–101
bathrooms, using accessible
    stall in, 108, 109
b/Blindness and blind people
    communicating with, 97
    National Federation of the
        Blind, 49
    offers to help, 103
    service dogs and, 95
    terms used when referring
        to, 14
Berkeley Center for Indepen-
    dent Living, 61
"bitter cripple" stereotype, 74
Black Panthers, 53
Black womanhood, 32
Blake, Melissa, 133
Blank, Wade, 54
brain injuries, 38
Bridges, Seven, 76

Brown, Keah, 122
Brown, Lydia X.Z., 13
Buck, Carrie, 46–47
bullying, 76
buses, wheelchair-
    accessible, 54
Bush, George H.W., 57

C

Califano, Joseph, 53–54
Cameron, Anita, 54–55, 57
Capitol Crawl, the (1990),
    56–57
caregivers, disabled people
    murdered by, 85
Carter, Jimmy, 53
Carter-Long, Lawrence, 9
Cassuto, Leonard, 132
Centers for Independent Living
    (CILs), 61
cerebral palsey, 34, 35, 98, 136,
    137, 138
Chamberlin, Judi, 67
charity model, 40
children, disability etiquette
    with, 111–14
chronic illnesses, 35
CILs. See Centers for Indepen-
    dent Living (CILs)
Claiborne, Loretta, 51
cleft palate, 5
"cognitively disabled person,"
    use of term, 25
Cokley, Rebecca, 22
combat fatigue, 49
communication, 96–100.
    See also talking about
    disability
    about someone's ableist
        behavior or language,
        115–17
communication disorders, 35
Community Mental Health Act
    (CMHA), 50
community mental health
    centers, 50
competence, presuming,
    100–101
condescension, 101
"confined to a wheelchair," 15
consumer movement (psychi-
    atric survivors move-
    ment), 66–67
Convention on the Rights of
    Persons with Disabilities
    (2012), 59
COVID-19 pandemic, 60, 85
"crazy," use of term, 20

Crenshaw, Kimberlé, 32
"cripple(d)," use of term, 23
"cross-disability" work, 61
"crutch," use of term, 20
cultural identity, and use of
    capitalization when
    referring to a disability,
    13, 14
cultural model, 40
curb cuts, 82
Curtis, Lois, 58

D

Dart, Justin Jr., 56, 57
Dart, Yoshiko, 56
dating apps, 90
d/Deafblind, communicating
    with someone who is, 98
deafness and d/Deaf
    community, 9
    communicating with, 97
    Deaf President Now (DPN)
        movement, 55–56
    person-first language vs.
        identity-first language
        used for, 14
    respecting personal space
        of, 97
Deaf President Now (DPN), 56
"deaf," use of term, 21
DeMarco, Nyle, 137
Department of Health,
    Education, and Welfare
    (HEW), 53
developmental disabilities. See
    also autism and autistic
    community; intellectual
    disabilities
    affects of, 35
    infantilization and, 100
    presuming competence
        with, 100–101
    Self-Advocacy Movement
        and, 64–65
    Special Olympics and, 51
    use of person-first
        language (PFL) for, 13
diagnoses, use of person-first
    language for, 14
"differently abled," 16, 17
digital communication
    technology, 59
disability(ies)
    acquired, 38
    as an identity, 30–31
    apparent (visible), 37
    as a "bad thing," 123, 130
    definitions, 8–10
    euphemisms for, 14–16

expressing prejudice
    as a, 76
    in the media. See media,
        disability in the
    models for understanding,
        38–41
    nonapparent (invisible), 37
    portrayed in the media. See
        media, disability in the
    reasons for demystifying,
        1–2
    shift in acceptance and
        understanding of, 2
    simulating, 145–46
    talking about. See talking
        about disability
    temporary, 38
    types of, 35–36
disability community.
    See also disabled people
    on ableism, 73–74
    different movements within
        the, 60–67
    history of. See history of
        disability
    individual experiences and
        perspectives within the,
        4–5, 74
    making ideas and expe-
        riences of disability
        accessible to others, 3
    use of term, 4
disability etiquette, 88–117
    acceptable questions, 91–93
    assumptions about
        disability status, 107–8
    for children, 111–14
    communication, 96–100
    don'ts, 100–111
    do's, 89–100
    the Golden Rule and, 88
    helping others, 101–4
    infantilization and, 100
    jokes and nosy questions,
        89–90
    offering advice, 91
    praying and, 106
    presuming competence
        and, 100–101
    respecting personal space,
        93–94
    staring and looking away,
        104–5
    stopping the cycle of poor,
        114–15
    touch and, 94–95
disability history. See history
    of disability

Disability Justice Movement, 62–63
disability rights activism
ADAPT, 54–55
Capitol Crawl (1990), 56–57
during the Great Depression, 47–48
Gang of 19, 54
Gaullaudet University protests, 55–56
HEW protests, 53–54
lawsuit against New York City Board of Education, 51
need for, 3
in the 1940s, 49
in the twenty-first century, 59–60
disability status, making assumptions about, 107–8
disabled people. *See also* disability community
advocating for themselves, 143–44
expectations of, 126–27
generalizations about, 101
living in institutions. *See* institutions/institutionalization
making ideas and experiences of disability accessible to others, 3
in the media. *See* media, disability in the
number of, worldwide, 1
passing the mic to, 144–45
privilege and, 32, 33
recognizing and crediting work of, 146–47
Disabled Veterans Rehabilitation Act (1943), 48
discrimination, 3. *See also* ableism
by airlines, 55
during Great Depression, 47–48
intersection of marginalized identities and, 34
physical exam for teacher certification, 51
wage, 48
Domino's Pizza, 73
Down syndrome, 16, 59, 137
Duckworth, Tammy, 59
"dumb," use of term, 20
dwarfism, 22, 26
dyslexia, referring to a person with, 14

E

economic model, 41
education
ableism in, 84
functioning labels in, 18–19
legislation, 52–53, 60
teaching history of disability in schools, 45
Education for All Handicapped Children Act (1975), 52
Eisenhower, Dwight D., 50
elevators, in subway systems, 71
Eloise, Marianne, 135
Emery, Crystal R., 33
empathy, 109–11
employment
amendments to Social Security and vocational rehabilitation laws, 50
discrimination, during Great Depression, 47–48
Fair Labor Standards Act of 1938, 48, 73
National Employ the Physically Handicapped Week, 48–49
privilege and, 33
sheltered workshops, 59, 73
employment-to-population ratio, 33
etiquette. *See* disability etiquette
eugenics, 46
euphemisms for *disability*, 16, 17
Evans, Dominick, 77
ex-patient movement (psychiatric survivors movement), 66–67
expectations of disabled people, portrayed in the media, 126–27

F

Fair Labor Standards Act (1938), 38, 72
Findlay, Carly, 105
504 Sit-In (1977), 53
Floyd, Kings, 96
"freaks" and freak shows, 45, 132–33
Freeman-Sheldon syndrome, 133
functioning labels, 18–19

G

Gallaudet University, 55–56
Gang of 19, 54

Ginsburg, Ruth Bader, 58
Giuffria, Angel, 137–38, 139
"gimp," use of term, 23
Golden Rule, the, 88
Great Depression, 47–48
Green Mountain Self-Advocates, 65
Grey's Anatomy, 133
Gurza, Andrew, 90

H

Haddad, Ryan J., 138
"handi-capable," 17
"handicapped," use of term, 10–11, 24
Harkin, Tom, 56
Harris, Leah, 67, 104
Hatch, Jenny, 59
healthcare, based on disability status and "pre-existing conditions," 60
hearing disabilities, 36. *See also* deafness and deaf community
hearing loss, 5, 37, 38
helping disabled people, 101–4, 127–28
Henderson, Lacey, 107
Heritage House nursing home, 54
Heumann, Judith, 51, 53, 54
HEW buildings, protests at, 53–54
"high functioning," use of term, 18, 19, 24
history, famous disabled people in, 44
history of disability. *See also* disability rights activism
before the 20th century, 45
in the 1950s, 50
in the 1960s, 50–51
in the 1980s, 54–56
in the 1990s, 56–58
eugenics and, 46–47
during the Great Depression, 47–48
highlights of the twenty-first century, 58–60
movements within, 60–67
required teaching in public schools, 45
Hlibok, Greg, 56
Holmes, Oliver Wendell Jr., 47
Hughes, Jessica M.F., 66
human rights model, 41
human rights violations, 52

I

ichthyosis, 105
identity(ies)
  disability as one's, 30–31
  factors related to
    disability, 31
  intersecting, 32, 33–35
  privilege and, 25, 32–33
identity-first language (IFL),
    11–14
"idiot," use of term, 20
"imbecile," use of term, 20
inaccessibility, 78–81, 82
income. *See* wages and wage
    discrimination
Independent Living Movement,
    61–62
Indiana, 46
Individuals with Disabilities
    Education Act (IDEA),
    52–53
infantilization, 100
"insane," use of term, 19, 20
inspiration porn, 123–29
institutions/institutionalization
  ableism and, 84
  independent living move-
    ment and, 61–62
  involuntary sterilization in,
    46–47, 62
  Olmstead decision and, 58
  self-advocacy movement
    and, 64
  Willowbrook State
    School, 52
insult, using *disability* as an,
    21–22
intellectual disabilities
  affects of, 36
  Community Mental Health
    Act (CMHA) and, 50
  infantilization and, 100
  Self-Advocacy Movement
    and, 64–65
  Special Olympics and, 51
  students with, in general
    education classes, 84
  talking down to people
    with, 100
  use of person-first
    language (PFL) for, 13
  use of *retarded* as insult
    to, 22
  words used when talking
    about, 25
interpreters, 78, 97–98
intersectionality, 32–35
involuntary sterilization, 46

J

Job Accommodation Network
    (JAN), 81–82
Johnson, Roland, 64
jokes and joking, 73, 89–90

K

Kahlo, Frida, 44
Katz-Hernandez, Leah, 59
Keelan-Chaffins, Jennifer, 57
Kennedy, John F., 50–51

L

Ladau, Ellen, 2, 9, 114–15, 120
Ladau, Marc, 2, 126–27
Liao, Christine, 97
"lame", use of term, 19, 20
language. *See* talking about
    disability; terminology;
    vocabulary
Larsen syndrome, 2, 5, 39, 120
League of the Physically
    Handicapped, 47–48
learning about disability(ies),
    141, 148–49
learning disabilities, 36
"learning disabled person",
    use of term, 25
Legorreta, Conchita
    Hernandez, 97
letter boards, 98
Lewis, Jerry, 129
Liao, Christine, 97
Liebowitz, Cara, 9
Lomax, Bradley, 53
Love on the Spectrum (Netflix
    series), 135
"low functioning," use of term,
    18, 19, 24
Luterman, Sara, 65–66

M

Mad Pride, 67
marginalized community/
    identities
  being an ally to, 141–43
  Disability Justice Movement
    and, 62–63
  intersection of multiple,
    32, 33–35
  privilege and, 32–33
McCoy McDeid, Reyma, 142
McKeon, Kayla, 16
media, disability in the, 120–39
  ableist depictions, 122
  in author's childhood,
    120–21
  disability used as punchline
    for jokes in, 73
  disabled actors in, 137–39
  inspiration porn in, 123–29
  lack of diversity and
    authentic representation
    in, 121–22
  pity porn in, 129–35
  positive portrayals in,
    136–37
Medicaid, 60
medical model perspective, 39
mental health disabilities, 36
mental illness(es)
  community mental health
    centers, 50
  National Mental Health Act
    of 1946, 49
  psychiatric survivors
    movement, 66–67
  stigmatized in the media,
    131–32
  words which are slurs
    against, 23, 26
"mentally challenged," 17
"mentally handicapped," 25
"mentally retarded," 25
Mental Retardation and Com-
    munity Mental Health
    Centers Construction Act
    (1963), 50
Mercado, Jillian, 137
"midget" ("M-word"), use of
    term, 22
Mingus, Mia, 63, 148
minimum wage, being paid
    less than, 48, 72
mistakes, recognizing and
    owning up to, 147–48
mobility equipment.
    See also wheelchair
  referring to someone by
    their, 15
  rideshare drivers refusing
    rides to people using, 84
models, disabled, 137
models for understanding
    disabilities, 38–41
"moron," use of term, 19
Moss, Haley, 135
movements, within disability
    community, 60–67
Moyes, Jojo, 130
muscular dystrophy,
    129–30, 137
Muscular Dystrophy Associa-
    tion (MDA), 129–30

N

National Council on Independent Living, 62
National Disability Employment Awareness Month, 49
National Employ the Physically Handicapped Week, 48–49
National Mental Health Act of 1946, 49
Neal, D'Arcee, 34–35
Ne'eman, Ari, 59
Netflix, 73, 135, 136
neurodivergent people, 25, 65, 66
neurodiversity movement, 65–66
neurological disorders, 36
neurotypical (people), 25, 65, 66
New York City Board of Education, 51
nonapparent (invisible) disabilities, 37–38, 80
nondisabled people
    on ableism, 73–74
    accessible amenities used by, 108–9
    on becoming disabled, 38
    being an ally to disabled people, 141–49
    etiquette used by. See disability etiquette
    kindness toward disabled people, portrayed as saintly, 127–28
    privilege of, 33
    use of term, 25
nothing about us without us, 143–44
nursing homes, 54, 61, 62. See also institutions/institutionalization

O

Obama, Barack, 59
objectification of people, 132
O'Connell, Ryan, 136
Olmstead decision, 58
Ortiz, Naomi, 145
Owens, Major, 56

P

Paralympic Games, 55
paralysis, 38
"paralyzed", use of term, 20

Paralyzed Veterans of America (PVA), 49
parental rights, 84
parents
    deemed unfit on basis of a disability, 84
    inheriting a disability from, 2
    responding to children's questions and comments, 113–14
parking, "accessible," 11, 27, 107, 108, 109
Patrick and Emmy Lou, 120–21
People First movement, 13
personal space, being mindful of, 93–95, 97, 99
person-first language (PFL), 11–14
Pervez, Noor, 18–19
Philip, Aaron, 137
physical disabilities
    affects of, 36
    media portrayals of, 121–22, 129–31
    National Employ the Physically Handicapped Week, 48–49
    words used a slur against, 23, 27
"physically challenged," 16, 17
Physically Disabled Students' program, University of California, Berkeley, 61
Pilgrims, disabled, 45
pity porn, 129–35
polio, 44, 51, 61
polling places, access to, 55
praying/prayer, 41, 106
privilege, 32–34, 63
protests
    504 Sit-In, 53–54
    against Gallaudet University, 55–56
    Gang of 19 (1978), 54
    against Works Progress Administration discrimination, 47–48
"psychiatrically disabled person", use of term, 26
psychiatric survivors movement, 66–67
P.T. Barnum's freak shows, 45
public transportation, 54, 71

Q

questions
    acceptable, 91–93

from children, 111, 112–14
    nosy and unnecessary, 90–91

R

racism, 76
Rehabilitation Act of 1973, 52
    Section 504, 53
religious model, 41
"retarded", use of term, 22
rideshare drivers, 84
Rivera, Geraldo, 52
Roberts, Ed, 61, 62
Robertson, Scott Michael, 59
romantic relationships, 134, 135
Roosevelt, Franklin Delano (FDR), 44, 47
Ruvolo, Maddy, 110

S

Schaeffer, Tarah, 121
schools. See education
Schuller, Pamela Rae, 105
Section 504, of Rehabilitation Act, 53
Segura, Tom, 73
Self-Advocacy Movement, 64–65
Self Advocates Becoming Empowered, 65
service dogs, 95
Sesame Street, 121
sexuality, 134–35
sheltered workshops, 59, 72
Shriver, Eunice Kennedy, 51
Sinclair, Jim, 66, 90–91
Sinclair Invalid, 63
sit-ins, 53–54
Sjunneson, Elsa, 98
"slow", use of term, 20
social justice movements, disability being excluded from, 76–77
social model perspective, 39–40, 72
Social Security Act (1935), 48
    amendments, 50
Social Security Disability Insurance (SSDI), 50
"spaz," use of term, 23
Spears, Britney, 131
Special (Netflix series), 136
"special-ed," use of term, 25
"special needs," use of term, 16, 17, 24
Special Olympics, 51
staring, 104–5

stereotypes, 3
  "bitter cripple," 74
  of Black, physically disabled man, 34
  disability as an insult perpetuating, 21–22
  of disability in the media, 122
  of helplessness and of being in need of help, 142
  of the tragic disabled person, 130–31
sterilization, forced, 46–47
stigma(s) and stigmatizing disability, 3
  adults modeling, 113
  disguised as religious belief, 106
  everyday words and, 19–23
  in medical mystery/dramas on television, 132–33
  of mental illness in the media, 131–32
stimming, 104–5
Stroker, Ali, 60
Stuart, Madeline, 137
"stupid," use of term, 20
stuttering, 98
subways, 71
Sweeney, Eva, 98
sympathy, 110
systemic ableism, 71. See also ableism

T

talking about disability, 10–27.
  See also terminology; vocabulary
  disability used as an insult, 21–22
  euphemisms for disability, 16–18
  everyday words rooted in disability stigma, 19–21
  functioning labels, 18–19
  identity-first language (IFL), 11–14
  mobility equipment and, 15
  person-first language (PFL), 11–14
  use of "handicapped," 10–11
  using the word, disability, 16, 18
talking to disabled people, 96–100
Taussig, Rebekah, 80–81
television shows, medical mystery and medical dramas on, 132–33

temporarily able-bodied, 38
temporary disabilities, 38
terminology. See also talking about disability; vocabulary
  euphemisms for disability, 16, 17
  functioning labels, 18–19
  "normal," 18
  terms to not use, 22–27
  terms to use, 24–27
  use of "handicapped," 10–11
  using the word, disability, 16, 18
TIME'S UP website, 77
Tiny Tim (A Christmas Carol), 130
touch(ing), 94–95, 97
Tourette syndrome, 105
tragedy, media portraying disability as a, 129–31
transportation, 54, 71
trope, media, 122
Truman, Harry S., 49
Tubman, Harriet, 44
Twenty-First Century Communications and Video Accessibility Act (2010), 59
"twice exceptional," use of term, 17

U

"Ugly Laws," 52
Ulta Beauty, 137
United Nations Office for Disaster Risk Reduction, 85
U.S. Access Board, 52
U.S. Supreme Court
  Domino's Pizza lawsuit and, 73
  on forced sterilization, 47
  Olmstead decision, 58

V

Vermont, 59
veterans, 45, 49, 55
Virdi, Jaipreet, 9
Virginia State Colony for Epileptics and Feebleminded, 46
visible (apparent) disabilities, 37
vision disabilities, 36, 78. See also b/Blindness and blind people

vocabulary.
  See also terminology
  removing ableist words from your, 143
  stigmatizing disability, 20–22
vocational rehabilitation (VR), 48, 50
Voting Accessibility for the Elderly and Handicapped Act of 1984, 55

W

wages and wage discrimination, 48, 72, 85
Weintraub, Liz, 10
wheelchair
  curb cuts and, 82
  etiquette about personal space and, 93–94, 99
  jokes/joking about, 89–90
  media's authentic portrayal of people in, 137
  questions asked about, 92
  referring to someone who uses a, 15, 26
  subway system and, 71
wheelchair-accessible buses, 54
"wheelchair-bound," 15
Willowbrook State School, New York, 52
Wilson, Elaine, 58
Women's March (2017), 76–77
Works Progress Administration, 47–48
World Down Syndrome Day, 59
World War II, 48, 49

Y

Young, Stella, 123, 124

Published in the United States by Ten Speed Press, an imprint of Random House,
a division of Penguin Random House LLC, New York.
www.tenspeed.com

Ten Speed Press and the Ten Speed Press colophon are registered trademarks of
Penguin Random House LLC.

Library of Congress Cataloging-in-Publication Data
    Names: Ladau, Emily, 1991- author.
    Title: Demystifying disability : what to know, what to say, and how to be
        an ally / Emily Ladau.
    Description: First edition. | Emeryville : Ten Speed Press, [2021] |
        Includes bibliographical references and index.
    Identifiers: LCCN 2020041583 (print) | LCCN 2020041584 (ebook) |
        ISBN 9781984858979 (trade paperback) | ISBN 9781984858986 (ebook)
    Subjects: LCSH: People with disabilities. | Discrimination against people
        with disabilities. | Disabilities.
    Classification: LCC HV3011 .L33 2021 (print) | LCC HV3011 (ebook) |
        DDC 305.9/08—dc23
    LC record available at https://lccn.loc.gov/2020041583
    LC ebook record available at https://lccn.loc.gov/2020041584

Trade Paperback ISBN: 978-1-9848-5897-9
eBook ISBN: 978-1-9848-5898-6

Printed in China

Pages 8, 30, 44, 70, 88, and 120: Illustrations by Tyler Feder.
Page 161: Author photograph by Rick Guidotti.

Editor: Kaitlin Ketchum | Production editor: Doug Ogan | Editorial assistant: Want Chyi
Designer: Sarah Rose Weitzman | Art directors: Isabelle Gioffredi and Betsy Stromberg
Production manager: Serena Sigona
Copyeditor: Kristi Hein | Proofreader: Carolyn Keating | Indexer: Beverlee Day
Publicist: Leilani Zee | Marketer: Monica Stanton

10 9 8 7 6

First Edition